The Presence of the Absent

Where live our most cherished (or painful) memories? Where are lodged those whom we loved (or dreaded) after they have departed? They inhabit, at least for a while, in a gray zone located between our self and our world, sometimes as internal reminiscences sometimes as strikingly vivid images detected and interacted by individuals and occasionally by whole collectives, as tenuous or as solid presences.

This book familiarizes us with six examples of individuals and families in therapy who live and interact with *the presence of their absent*, pivotal people in their lives who either died or disappeared, but are still there. It familiarizes us with their plight in a tender, compassionate style, describing in detail interviews and therapeutic transformations and, in several cases, follow-ups as well as echoes of those processes. It teaches us to respect those presences as well as how to help families and individuals treasure them, and in many cases to let them go.

Written in a vivid, intense language, *The Presence of the Absent* offers a marvelous insight into these processes that may prove transformative for the therapist (both family and individually oriented), as well as enlightening to the general public.

Carlos E. Sluzki, MD is Professor Emeritus of Global and Community Health and of Conflict Analysis and Resolution at George Mason University, and Professor (Clinical) of Psychiatry and Behavioral Sciences at George Washington University School of Medicine. He is an internationally renowned psychiatrist and family therapist who trained in both Argentina and the United States.

The Presence of the Absent

Therapy with Families and their Ghosts

Carlos E. Sluzki

Routledge
Taylor & Francis Group

NEW YORK AND LONDON

First published 2016
by Routledge
711 Third Avenue, New York, NY 10017

and by Routledge
27 Church Road, Hove, East Sussex BN3 2FA

Routledge is an imprint of the Taylor & Francis Group, an informa business

Library of Congress Cataloging-in-Publication Data
Sluzki, Carlos E., author.
The presence of the absent : therapy with families and their ghosts /
Carlos E. Sluzki.
p. ; cm.
Includes bibliographical references and index.
I. Title.
[DNLM: 1. Family Therapy—methods. 2. Attitude to Death.
3. Culturally Competent Care. 4. Family Relations. 5. Hallucinations.
6. Professional-Patient Relations. WM 430.5.F2]
RC488.5
616.89'156—dc23
2014049492

ISBN: 978-1-138-84779-8 (hbk)
ISBN: 978-1-138-84778-1 (pbk)
ISBN: 978-1-315-72650-2 (ebk)

Typeset in Berkeley
by Swales & Willis Ltd, Exeter, Devon, UK

Printed and bound in the United States of America by Publishers Graphics,
LLC on sustainably sourced paper.

Contents

About the Author vi
Acknowledgments viii
Foreword, by Salvador Minuchin x

1 Ethereal Presences 1

2 Forbidden Words, Forbidden Thoughts: Semantic and
   Somatic Effects of Political Repression in a Family with
   a Hole in its Center 10

3 Rekindling the Experience of Freedom: Ghosts of
   a Dictatorship and Reverberations in a Liberating Process 34

4 House Taken Over: Culture, Migration and Developmental
   Cycle in a Moroccan Family Overtaken by Ghosts 45

5 The Ancient Cult of Madame: When Therapists Trade
   Curiosity for Certainty 68

6 The Naming: The Awakening of Two Ghost Children 80

7 *Saudades* at the Edge of the Self and the Merits of
   "Portable Families" 89

8 Wrap Up 100

References 105
Index 110

About the Author

Carlos E. Sluzki, MD, was born and raised in Buenos Aires, Argentina, where he graduated from medical school and was trained in psychiatry and in psychoanalysis. In turn, he was trained in family therapy at the Mental Research Institute (MRI), Palo Alto, California, during the early days of that discipline.

In 1972 Dr. Sluzki migrated to the United States with a prestigious John S. Guggenheim Foundation Fellowship. Since then his career has included being Director of Training and later Director of the above-mentioned MRI (1976–1983) as well as Professor of Psychiatry at the University of California San Francisco (1975–1983), at the University of Massachusetts Medical School (1983–1993), and at the University of California Los Angeles (1993–2003). Dr. Sluzki resides currently in Washington, DC, where he is Clinical Professor of Psychiatry at George Washington University School of Medicine and Professor Emeritus of Global and Community Health and of Conflict Analysis and Resolution at George Mason University. Dr. Sluzki has been Editor-in-Chief of the journals *Acta Psiquiatrica y Psicologica de America Latina*, *Family Process*, and the *American Journal of Orthopsychiatry*, and Vice-President of the American Family Therapy Association. He is a twice awardee of the American Family Therapy Academy, a Distinguished Life Fellow of the American Psychiatric Association and of the American College of Psychiatrists, and a honorary member of multiple professional organizations in the United States, Latin America, Asia, and Europe.

He has published extensively—including more than 200 articles in professional journals, book chapters and books, including *The Double Bind: Foundation of the Communicational Approach to the Family* (with Donald Ransom) and his recent *The Social Network, Frontier of the Systemic Practice*. Dr. Sluzki has also been actively involved in human rights and the plight of refugees/IDPs, has been consultant to the World Health Organization and to the Office of the Prosecutor of the International Criminal Court, has received multiple awards and delivered countless keynote and panel presentations and conducted workshops worldwide, with special emphasis on family therapy, social networks, violence and victimization, refugees and human rights (www.sluzki.com).

Acknowledgments

Chapters 3, 4, 5, and 7 evolved from articles previously published in professional journals, listed below. I acknowledge with appreciation those journals for their authorization to utilize that material as a base for the corresponding chapters.

Sluzki, C.E. (1990). "Disappeared: Semantic and somatic effects of political repression in a family seeking therapy." *Family Process*, 29(2): 131–143.

Sluzki, C.E. (1997). "Rekindling the experience of freedom: From the personal to the collective . . . and back." *Human Systems*, 8(3–4): 225–238.

Sluzki, C.E. (2004). "A house taken over by ghosts: Culture, migration and developmental cycle in a Moroccan family invaded by hallucinations." *Families, Systems and Health*, 22(3): 321–337.

Sluzki, C.E. (2008). "The ancient cult of madame: When therapists trade curiosity for certainty." *Journal of Family Therapy (UK)*, 30: 119–130.

Sluzki C.E. (2008). "*Saudades* at the edge of the self and the merits of portable families" *Transcultural Psychiatry*, 45: 379–390.

I also wish to express my gratitude to these and many other families, couples, and individuals whom I accompanied, and who accompanied me, in the course of my professional practice. They incorporated me temporarily as a meaningful member of their social network, and allowed me to dive into their stories—stories that ended up inhabiting a space that included me—while opening up to my contributions, sometimes incorporating them into their worldview and sometimes wisely questioning my premises. In doing so they taught me many things about life, suffering, rebuilding, hope and joy, about my fallibility while occasionally validating my capacity to help them to introduce changes in their lives. This recursive process of learning and helping to learn, of changing and helping to change, has been and is for me an ever-present source of nourishment.

Likewise, my heartfelt appreciation to mentors, colleagues, and friends who have oriented, expanded and enriched both my personal and my professional life and contributed to its evolution at different moments of my journey. Looking backwards, a few shine with special light: Mauricio Goldenberg, Eliseo Veron, Paul Watzlawick, Virginia Satir, Don D. Jackson, Janet Helmick Beavin, Heinz von Foerster, Gianfranco Cecchin, Elida Romano, Julio Aranovich, and Donald A. Bloch. To them, and to many other colleagues and friends with whom I shared and share community, my love and my debt.

I wish also to express my deep appreciation for colleagues and friends who at different moments provided me with constructive suggestions in the process of writing this book. Special thanks are due to my beloved wife and personal and intellectual companion, Sara Cobb, PhD, for her solid stimulation and warm support and for the many ideas conveyed in many conversations and in her admirable book *Speaking of Violence* (Cobb, 2013); to my admired senior colleague, creative pioneer and generous friend Salvador Minuchin for his kind prologue and for so much more; to my friend Saul Malozowski, MD for his detailed review and feedback of this book while in progress; and, of course, to the late Gabriel Garcia Marquez, Nobel Prize of Literature, who brought forth magic realism and validating that dimension through the esthetic door, thus bringing it out of the closet of our private if not secret world into the light of our explicit daily experiences.

CES
Washington, DC.

Foreword

Salvador Minuchin

This book should be read twice: the first time for the pure esthetic enjoyment of Dr. Sluzki's mastery of the short story narrative; the second to reflect on the meaning of his writing about the nature of the human condition and the process of change.

As I read his cases, I often felt that I was listening to a wise man that had traveled along many roads, reflecting on other cultures and on the consequences of his work. He invites us to revisit a situation from his early career, for instance, when he treated a psychotic patient with a delusional system about saving the world. With antipsychotic drugs, the man improved, lost his voices, became depressed—and killed himself. The memory of that case seems to permeate the approach to other situations: "Don't kill the dream; it may hurt the dreamer."

In all these true stories, this wise expert takes a path that is unexpected. Working with a Moslem immigrant family where multiple members have nightmares and visions of frightening images, Sluzki engages them in interesting conversations about the magic power of dreaming, the differences between good and bad dreams, and the meanings in the Koran about the effects of dreaming. There is nothing in their discussion about the effects of immigration; cultural clashes among generations; the nature of family organization, with its rigid hierarchical structure; or the position of women. We learn about the invisible question marks in the head of the therapist when he guides us to reflect with him. The session seems a conversation among friendly neighbors, the therapist always respectful and curious, helping family members to expand the range of their own narratives. He lets them leave in order to continue to expand their conversation, unaware that Sluzki's voice goes with them.

While Sluzki is clearly influenced by the narrative school of family therapy, his therapy is highly idiosyncratic. Joining with the family, he lets himself be entrapped by their narrative, meandering through strange territories, paying close attention to details, and adding a slightly discordant chord, where he can, that introduces ambiguity into the family story. The interference is friendly, familiar, respectful and optimistic. He believes the family has resources they can utilize, and he lends them his hope. Sluzki reminds me of a Borges story, where the traveler comes to a crossroad and is invited to take both paths. He chooses one, but he hears the echo of his steps walking on the road not taken. The style is minimalist, the influence invisible but powerful.

In some situations, the message "Don't kill the dream" is expanded, suggesting, rather, "Cultivate your dreams; they bring forth changes that you may want to accept." That message is richly illustrated in his work with an old woman, who came to therapy accompanied by her two dead sons. In this situation, he focused on advising her how to teach the sons about her right of privacy. Other situations are more complex, involving many levels of social, political, relational, and individual trauma. In such a case, we see the skill of Sluzki in dealing with the destructive effects of a despotic political regime, which has demanded that victims and witnesses alike must abolish their memories. Two years later, when an audience from the same culture viewed the session, they were all captured by the memory of that fear, and by their fear of remembering.

Carlos Sluzki is an astute political observer and committed activist. His analysis of this case demonstrates how a master clinician with such an orientation can use the description of a family story to illustrate a universe of shadows.

In this book, Dr. Sluzki has thrown a pebble into a social lake. Please look at the expanding circles.

Ethereal Presences

Yo no creo en brujas, pero que las hay, las hay.[1]

(Spanish saying)

Our beloved talking cat, an agile acrobat and tender social being, would jump onto my desk whenever I was there and managed to create a space to lie down by pushing away whatever paper, pen, or stapler was in his way and purr until falling asleep. He would climb onto the window pane in my studio and look at me while calling imperiously until I opened it for him to go out and explore the garden again. He followed my wife and I throughout the house, parking himself in whatever room of our choosing without demands, without asking to be petted, just being there for the sheer joy of sharing the space in good company. This cherished member of our household died two months ago hit by a car while crossing the street during one of his incursions into the neighbor-hood. Weeks after his death, reeling from his loss, I still quasi-hallucinate him: every now and again I have the sense of seeing his shadow outside my studio window wanting to be allowed into the house after one of his escapades; or I experience him rushing in or out when I enter the house. Slowly and steadily, at his own pace and mine, he is erasing himself from the world of the present and into the bittersweet world of the memories of the lost loved ones.

What a fascinating process is such a transition, a road frequented by so many of our objects of love that are no longer physically present, inaccessible to our sight, hearing, smelling, touching, and to our experience of being touched by them, but lingering just the same for a while! Far from being a cognitive experience ("Presto, maestro! Let's make them disappear!"), letting go of those no longer with us is a laborious process—akin to the developmental cycle of a ghost limb in an amputee[2]—in which our senses trick us, probably to help us learn the painful experience of letting go.

Our social world is populated by people of flesh and bones and souls, accessible to us *in vivo* in our daily life, or at least available through the reliable technology of intermediary objects such as fixed or cellular phones and internet devices, and through the fading retro method of mail correspondence, preceded in its progressive obsolescence by the already disappeared use of telegrams. This quality of "tangible presence" is also shared by a variety of extra-human social substitutes, especially our domestic animals—and, when children, our dolls, teddy bears, and the sort, whom we anthropomorphize and incorporate into our stable network of relations: we talk to them at length as if they could understand us and even may invite them to share our solitary bed, enjoying their attachment when they lean against us, considering those acts as solid proof that somebody out there loves us—regardless of whether many of those behaviors fade away once we grow up (or, in the case of some pets, once we have fed them!).

In a constructionist definition proposed in a pre-systemic, pre-constructionist world, Enrique Pichon-Riviere (formulated in 1960, cited in 2001), a pioneering Argentine social psychiatrist and psychoanalyst, defined the *self* as a dialectical amalgam of our self-reflected view of our own mind, of our body, and of our micro- as well as macro-social environment. Within that composite we strive to differentiate what is part of our "internal world," the world of emotions, cognitions, memories, and imagination from the world that surrounds us, the "external world," that is, whatever is perceived by our distant senses—the eyes and the ears—and eventually by our proximate senses—the touch, the smell, the taste—as beyond the boundary of our skin. At the same time, the external world contributes to a process of constant revision of that constructed self by means of the behaviors of the other, captured in that "spiral of reciprocal perspectives" that includes their view of us tinted by their view of our view of them, in turn affected by our views of their view of our view of them and so on, *ad nauseam* (Laing, Phillipson, & Lee, 1972).

Time and time again these confines of the self prove to be supple and surprisingly mobile, if not arbitrary. An inattentive driver mildly hits at our car while we are in it, or we do it ourselves in a moment of distraction, and we wince as if our body would have hurt. Someone insults a person dear to us our—our child, our mate, our friend—and we react emotionally and physically as if the affront would have been a physical act directed at us. The burning of their flag, the desecration of their temple, or the mocking of their deity by caricature and video ushers forth in many a reaction of fury, as if it would imply a deep personal affront. Cars, parents, children, flags, and temples are lodged within the ever-mutating frontiers of our self.

Many other circumstances and conditions may contribute to blur these boundaries. To start with, somebody near and dear to us dies, or abandons us, and we retain for a while the experience of their presence—we talk to them, we have the impression that they are still there, occupying a physical space, we even sense that we saw them in the street or that they are in the adjacent room—to slowly but surely fade away with the passage of time and the painful process of mourning, until they yield their presence as a ghost[3] to become a memory.

But many other events may contribute to populate our world with these ghosts. We are captured by a nightmare and may wake up, still under its spell, struggling to differentiate between what was a dream and what belongs to the world of the awakened. We have high fever, and we may find ourselves surrounded by visions, sometimes fuzzy and sometimes very clear, sometimes horribly scary and sometimes friendly. We are hospitalized to break the vicious cycle of chronic alcohol abuse, and the agitation and extreme distress of a delirium tremens may be made more terrifying by the vampires and insects that invade our room, when not entertained by a jazz band of Lilliputian homunculi sitting on the candelabra of our room.[4] We enter into ecstasy after hours of praying repetitively or dancing frenetically in homage to our god, and soon, we see and hear a choir of angels or, if we are part of a Brazilian Candomblé cult, find a Yoruba-Catholic syncretic god-saint piggybacking on us and we enter in a profoundly altered state of consciousness. We smoke a strong toke of marijuana, or ingest LSD, and we fuse with a generally peaceful and occasionally scary universe, without a clear notion of where our body ends and where the surroundings begin. We chew some *ayahuasca* mushroom in the Peruvian Amazon and the most incredible creatures begin to materialize around us. We do it with peyote in Sonora, Mexico, and, in no time, those spirits that years ago visited Castaneda (1968) and his Yaqui mentor-guide, Don Juan, share their teachings with us. Or we simply get distracted and may have the sense that we have traveled through time and space, as characters of *One Hundred Years of Solitude* (Garcia Marquez, 1967) do in the fictitious town of Macondo with so much grace and suppleness.

Of course, if we happen to live in a culturally homogeneous region where our group of reference—extended family, friends, neighbors—see and hear with reasonable frequency menacing or friendly creatures in the night, including perhaps people already dead that we still miss, we take for granted the permeable nature of those boundaries and we partake in these experiences. These ghosts—with different degrees of materiality—may appear in the evening twilight to teach us a lesson, or scare us, or provide consolation for our loss, assuring us that their journey to the netherworld has been peaceful, or forgive us for the unavoidable paradoxical ambivalence of many mourning processes, namely, their accompanying secret relief that we are still alive (Paul, 1986).

Even in our materialistic, complex occidental culture, we, sophisticated people raised in a milieu striving to establish a thicker boundary between the "real" and the "imaginary," may have to acknowledge that our social world includes virtual presences, ghosts, specters, and other invisible companions. They are sometimes benevolent and welcomed, as the "many voices" of colleagues that converse with, or are enacted through, my distinguished prefacer, Salvador Minuchin (1987) in the course of his clinical practice, as happens with so many of us. But on occasions they can also be malignant incubi that we try to scare away with distractions or secret rituals. We may interact with them fluidly, taking their presence in our daily life for granted, or they may catch us by surprise and invade us with their presence. They may reach us through our senses, clearly and unambiguously, or tenuously, as vague presences. We may not even realize that they are there until becoming aware of their presence by a trace that they left while passing by, or by the virtual space that they seem to occupy in our surroundings. These materializations are mostly kept as private, intimate, secret contacts, and seldom experienced as anomalies.

Occasionally, our commitment to these ghosts, or our stubborn struggle against them, escalates to the point of occupying a good part of our attention and energy. If a combination of genetic proclivity and environmental conditions dictate, at a given moment of our life, we may hear mumbling voices referring to us in menacing ways, sense utterances or special meanings transmitted through the television, or mysteriously believe that a micro-receptor has been implanted in the center of our brain by the KGB or CIA or the extraterrestrials. In these circumstances, whether locked in battle against them or extremely engaged with them at the expense of the routines of our lives, this radical shift in our behavior may call the attention of our family or of authorities in charge of maintaining public order, and we may end up having a psychiatrist diagnosing us as suffering from schizophrenia or the like, a label easier to stick on than to peel off once stuck.[5]

A variety of experiences of this sort, some more unusual than others, some subtle and some massive, invading individuals, family groups, and even crowds, will be detailed in this book.

Any therapeutic interview—and up to a point any complete set of therapeutic encounters (any "treatment") with an individual, a couple, or a family—can be analyzed by observing it as a whole, or by dissecting it into generic components.

The "*whole*" entails discussions on style, ethics and esthetic of the process, as well as speculations about what moments are pivotal in the shifts or consolidation of the narratives that are presented and evolving throughout it. The generic components include, amoung others:

- *the nature of the intake process*, from the first phone call of a family member requesting a consultation, including the interaction between the caller and the intake person, and the early and subsequent interactions with the therapist focused on data gathering, intertwined with;
- *the joining process*, namely, the ongoing relational negotiation—both explicit and implicit—between therapist and patients about the nature of relationship, reciprocal expectations of process and outcomes, and issues related to boundaries and trust;
- *the intriguing relationship between the "opening moves", (whatever is stated or enacted at the beginning of a session) and the text (whatever happen next, what is brought as focus of the conversation by those who consult)*, that is, the relationship between the telling first moves at the opening of the consultation and/or of a session—who says and does what, how do they display their issues—and the narratives about the nature and causes of the problem as well as its evolution throughout the treatment;
- *the therapeutic process* proper, that is, the progressive transformation of what is defined as problems or dilemmas and their solutions or dissolutions throughout the therapeutic conversation (i.e., the evolution of the problematic narratives into "well-formed" stories that redistribute assets, increase resourcefulness and, hopefully, constructively transform if not dissolve conflicts);
- *the anchoring* of key reformulations and of useful alternative views, that is, how the therapist consolidates them at crucial moments throughout the interview, including the closure of the consultation, and of the treatment;
- *the therapist's style and frame of reference*, namely, the personal style as well as the theory and ethics of practice underlying the therapist's actions and inactions throughout the consultation;
- and, just to leave a healthy open "waste basket" category to be filled by the reader, *many other possible variables and observables.*

Some of these variables can be traced only when a session is observed *in vivo*, behind a one-way screen or in close circuit, in a videotaped interview and, up to a point, when reading a verbatim transcript, such as the consultation detailed in Chapter 4. Others will be highlighted in the text interspersed with the narratives about consultations and treatments—including hybrids of narratives and transcriptions, as is the case of consultations discussed in Chapters 2, 5, 6, and 7, or when the narrative of the consultation is based on notes made after the session rather than by video or audio recordings.

While my own discussion of these different events are generally focused on one or at the most two of these variables, I list them above to invite the readers to choose additional sets of observables—the global gestalt or some discrete set of variables—to further enrich their experience while reading these consultations, as well as in the review of material from their own practices.

Chapter 2, "Forbidden Words, Forbidden Thoughts: Semantic and Somatic Effects of Political Repression in a Family with a Hole in its Center," focuses on the admission interview and a brief course of therapy with a family of seven— five of them present in the transcribed session, while two of them, key adults in that family constellation, were "*desaparecidos*," people swallowed by the repressive apparatus of a military *de facto* government that was in power at that time in Argentina. The chapter briefly describes that political context, details the admission interview with this family, and summarizes seven subsequent sessions of treatment. This is followed by a discussion of the effects of the oppressive political climate on the family's language, social adaptation, and health, and of the goals of therapy with families of absent-but-present members of which the *desaparecidos* are paradigmatic.

Chapter 3, "Rekindling the Experience of Freedom: Ghosts of a Dictatorship and Reverberations in a Liberating Process," shifts gears toward collective presences. It describes the catalytic effect of presenting the family situation discussed in the previous chapter to a professional audience of therapists attending a family therapy congress that took place as the military dictatorship mentioned above was being replaced by a democratically elected government, while its oppressive injunctions were still in the air. The presentation re-activated in good part the audience fears and protective moves emanating from the persistent after-effect of threats and negative injunctions emanating from that regime, to then becoming witness of their own liberation from them. The discourse of this chapter is perhaps more militant and less intimate than that of the other chapters of this book, and reminds us with vigor about the expanding, reciprocally influencing circles of contexts, as well as the political nature of all clinical practice.

Chapter 4, "House Taken Over: Culture, Migration and Developmental Cycle in a Moroccan Family Overtaken by Ghosts," details the interview with a large family whose central characters, the paterfamilias and his silent wife, migrated years before from the North African Magreb to an industrial city of France. They were living, however, in an ethnic neighborhood and maintained many habits of their country of origin, creating a micro-world of extreme dissonance from that of their country of adoption, forcing an unavoidable cultural struggle with special impact on the life of their offspring. Not surprisingly, this family and its conflict provide a prime example of the assumption that whatever necessary task of cultural adaptation is not accomplished by the first generation of immigrants will be accomplished in spades by the second generation. The interview evolves mainly in a supple language populated by dreams, nightmares, and hallucinations, to end gently with a de-labeling of that son—who was at risk of suffering the added injury of a psychiatric diagnosis—as well as a seed for a reconnection between father and son (and a bridging between cultural expectations) that, according to follow-up information, seemed to be holding.

Chapter 5, "The Ancient Cult of Madame: When Therapists Trade Curiosity for Certainty," begins with details of a painful experience that slapped the face of this author early in his professional career, when his good-intentioned while naive *furor sanandi* led to a tragic end. This anecdote is evoked as a frame for the presentation and discussion of six sessions of treatment with a family whose social world includes the virtual but dominant presence of one of its key members, already dead for five years. As it turned out, the strength of the presence of this ghost (and its pervasive interactive materialization by them) clashed with the therapist's intentions to liberate the family from the presence of that hegemonic being. Further—a realization by hindsight—the struggle to do so exceeded the needs and expectation of the family members, ultimately requiring a shift of focus and of goals. This is followed by a discussion about potential problems caused when the therapist becomes mesmerized and, to a point, captivated (i.e., captured) by a family story. This fascination may be epistemologically discontinuous from, if not contradictory to, Gianfranco Cecchin's (1987) wise recommendation toward cherishing a stance of permanent "curiosity" as a central dictum in therapy.

Chapter 6, "The Naming: The Awakening of Two Ghost Children," centers on a consultation with a couple about a lingering post-partum depression in the wife after giving birth to a healthy, lively daughter, while carrying in the shadows of their shared emotional memory the burden of an unfinished business with a prior birth-related drama. The consultation evolves very smoothly, with the consultant asking only very few targeted questions that unleash an emotional storm and an "exorcism" of sorts. The relationship between fragmented stories and past traumas is then discussed, as well as other issues about the construction of narratives.

Chapter 7, "*Saudades* at the Edge of the Self, and the Merits of 'Portable Families,'" focuses on the treatment of an older Mexican-American woman who was referred to the author due to hallucinations that her previous psychiatrist defined as a symptom of schizophrenia but who was frustratingly unresponsive to anti-psychotic medication. A culturally attuned conversation with this lady revealed a world of "magic realism" that is far from infrequent in elderly people with a small and dwindling social network, especially if coming from cultures with fuzzy boundaries between the inner and the outer world. Respecting those traits allowed for the development of treatment approaches that evolved satisfactorily without disrupting the patient's comfortable inscription in this dual world, inhabited by selected members of the netherworld.

Chapter 8, "Wrap Up," as any epilogue, bites the tail of the beginning of this book, revising common patterns and musing about this and that.

It should be underlined that none of these phenomena are treated here as "pathology." In fact, conceiving them as pathological would undermine one of the basic premises that have guided my clinical work and the consultations that I detail in all these chapters, namely, that what we call reality varies with circumstances and culture. While those experiences may appear as unusual to us, a good part of the engaging process within the world of those who experience them consists of our acknowledging these realities, familiarizing with them, and treating them respectfully. Should we challenge them? Only on occasions, when we are asked to, and sometimes—and very carefully—when these virtual presences demonstrate having the toxic quality of reducing the degrees of freedom in those that trust in us to increase it.

So, in the pages that follow, the reader will be introduced to worlds that include the stable familiar presence of those who are neither alive nor dead (an almost unavoidable impact of an "ambiguous loss" [see discussion on pp. 29–32]), of the pervasive menacing voices of oppression and terror, of terrifying struggles between angels and furious dogs as well as flying medusas, of invisible bodies and virtual cults, of faithful and soothing dead sons. We will also witness the challenge to detect and befriend these presences, and, on occasion, to entice them to let go.

Notes

1 "I don't believe in witches, but they surely exist."
2 Which for some is a permanent feature and for others they progressively fade away or, in an experience perceived by them as bizarre, the ghost forearm, arm or leg slowly telescopes inwards, so the last one to disappear from the proprioceptive perception is a hand or a foot, attached to the stump.
3 The word "ghost" in the subtitle of this book as well as abundantly throughout these pages is used quite liberally—rather than literally—in reference to persistent sensorial presences— sometimes perceived as good, sometimes as evil, and sometimes neither—that, while perceived or enacted by individuals, occasionally family groups and not infrequently communities under special circumstances and even whole cultural collectives, are privileged in the sense of not shared by external third parties.
4 While not having seen homunculi or listened to their music proper, I bore witness to such an event during my hospital practice, where a patient with a florid delirium tremens was having a great time wittnessing and describing vividly that spectacle from his hospital bed.

And this is a good opportunity to add an endnote to this endnote as I use here—and I will use with some frequency in the rest of this book—a word that, at least in the United States, has been criticized by some as "politically incorrect," namely, "patient." "Patient," traditionally used to denote whomever occupies the role of those who consult a professional in the healing arts, has lost some *gravitas* mainly as a result of the strategic efforts of managed health-care companies, which have pumped up the alternative usage of the label "client" and, as a counterpart, the one of unspecific "provider" (while those organizations infiltrated themselves inbetween both and acquired political and economic power). This semantic slight of hands was sustained, in an unwilling alliance, by the supporters of the progressive belief that the relation between healer (psychiatrist, psychologist, clinical social worker, counselor, nurse practitioner, and so on) and patient needed to be cleansed from its potentials and frequently enacted oppressive power nature. In order not to throw the baby of semantic clarity out with the bathwater of the economic advantages of managed care organizations, I retain the word "patient," while acknowledging its potential political shortcoming (for more on this, see Sluzki, 2000.)

5 Juan Marconi, an influential Chilean public health psychiatrist with whom I interacted frequently during the 1960s, conducted an ethnographic study at the main psychiatric hospital for women in Santiago, Chile. The disproportionately large number of Mapuche Indians among its inmates alarmed him. He was able to unveil a common pathway for most of them: an illiterate Mapuche-speaking woman would come to the capital city to work as a house servant, or to visit a family member; if the address of their destination (frequently written in a piece of paper and given to them for the travel) was incomplete or inaccurate, they would become disoriented and lost in the big city. Unable to find their destination, they entered into a trance, a state of agitation and dream-like hallucinations, as is habitual in their own milieu, where it would immediately elicit help and reassurances. Further unable to explain their predicament in their extremely rudimentary Spanish, they would be labeled as psychotic and hospitalized accordingly, where they would be kept for prolonged periods because their "symptoms" did not improve (Muñoz, Marconi, Horwirz, & Naveillan, 1966). It took Marconi and his disciples some strong public health advocacy to begin to revert that trend. It pre-dates, and resonates very closely indeed with, Rosenhan's (1973) indictment in "Being sane in insane places"!

Forbidden Words, Forbidden Thoughts: Semantic and Somatic Effects of Political Repression in a Family with a Hole in its Center

2

This chapter transcribes and comments on a family interview that I facilitated in Argentina in 1983, in the socio-political context of the waning period of a violently repressive military government in power at that time. The family interviewed was, in fact, one of the many victims of the actions of that dictatorial regime. Two members of this family were detained and "disappeared" already several years before, and their parental functions had since been occupied by other family members. Their ambiguous status (Are they dead or alive?) and the tenacity of the presence of threats voiced by the captors and, ultimately, by the machinery of the State, created a toxic combination of silence and mystifications that froze the evolution of this family while unleashing in them a panoply of somatic symptoms.

The "disappeared" couple were a permanently present void in the center of this family—involved in a shroud of narrative mystification and secrecy. Equally present was the repressive apparatus of the State, materialized for this family in the threat made by the leader of the armed team that had kidnapped the couple: if they would mention to anybody their disappearance, the couple's fate would be sealed. That threat was followed by a denial of any knowledge of the operative on the part of any official authorities that was subsequently contacted by the family—the police, the military, the ecclesiastic hierarchy—which confirmed the total impunity with which the military government could operate, and gave added validity to the threat and strength of the silence. As a result, this family had organized its whole life at the obedient service of these injunctions, avoiding mentioning their predicament in their meager relational world and, in fact, avoiding as much as possible any social contact with the outer world. The emotional and social effect on this family (and in a sizeable part of the general population in that country) of this context of oppression and of mystifying incompatible messages ("We kidnapped them but don't know anything about them") was devastating.

The repressive practices that led to the "disappearance"[1] of tens of thousands of citizens in Argentina during the period of the military dictatorship lasting from 1976 to 1983 generated an impact that evokes a sentence previously utilized in reference to the Holocaust: words fail in their descriptive power. In fact, systematic political carnage—from the Inquisition to the Khmer Rouge, from Auschwitz-Birkenau to the Gulag, from the Rwandan genocide to Pinochet's Chile to the Argentina of the *desaparecidos*—generates what has been described as aporia, a philosophical impasse characterized by the inability to comprehend ("How is it possible that human beings . . . ?"). Violence of such a magnitude destroys the capacity to generate a story, to provide a coherent narrative. Paraphrasing Elaine Scarry (1985)—who was referring specifically to the effects of torture—the violence by the State actively destroys the language and the normative world not only of the victims but also of the third parties, of their families and, ultimately, of the general population, all victims of the oppression of that victimization.

Contributing to this paralysis was the already mentioned *ambiguous loss* (Boss, 2006), namely, the simultaneous emotional presence and physical absence of the "disappeared" in their family. To that should be added the family's double-binding compulsion to obey the injunction not to mention their situation in any public setting, even while in many circumstances—the children's school, their few friends, their neighbors, even the therapeutic context in which this consultation was taking place—that absence was obvious, and very present. They would talk about this, of course, between them in the privacy of their home, but the disappeared were referred to sometimes in present tense and sometimes in past tense, always ambiguously.[2] In sum, the mystification of their reality was pervasive, invading the realm of the public and the private spheres, the social and the intimate.

The Political Context: A Brief Synopsis

The military regime that established itself as the government in Argentina after the 1976 *coup d'état* unleashed an internal repressive apparatus that constituted a model of what is called state terrorism. Arguing the need to truncate an urban guerilla movement that had appeared in the Argentine political scene as a reaction to the betrayal of promises made by their prior old leader, Juan Peron— by then recently deceased—and expanding an already active paramilitary death squad supported by the State already in action since 1970, the new *de facto* government unleashed a "dirty war" (a term used by the government itself) as a "final solution" to subversion (see, among others, Corradi, 1985; Graziano, 1992). Between 1976 and 1982, relying on power and impunity and guided by a bloody messianic official discourse, military operatives abducted from their homes or their workplace an estimated 15,000 to 30,000 persons, who were subsequently tortured and killed—a few others were let go after torture and expelled from the country. Those actions had the aim of eliminating any opponents while creating a climate of terror that would quash any voice of dissent. Some of the victims were actual militants in clandestine armed groups, but the vast majority were active students, union leaders, intellectuals, journalists, people mentioned in torture sessions by others, or simply persons being in the wrong place at the wrong time—eliminating in that way, the militaries argued, those suspected of "future subversion." At the same time, the official response to any inquiry about the whereabouts of those kidnapped individuals was to deny any knowledge of their abduction. They were the *desaparecidos,* the vanished ones. The deterrent effect of these policies on the general population was efficient and enduring. The main consistent voice of grief and grievance, made louder by the surrounding silence, came from a grassroots organization called Madres de Plaza de Mayo (Plaza de Mayo being the square flanking the government house, where on a daily basis mothers and other female relatives of *desaparecidos* would walk in silence with posters with the names and photos of those who were unaccounted for).[3] Their consistent, dramatic, silent weekly presence, in spite of harassment by police and by media and of ridicule by the official communiqués, contributed to keeping the issue alive and to maintaining in the public eye and conscience that collective murder as well as the government's impunity and unaccountability. Torture/killing centers (340 countrywide, according to the data provided during the trials of those dictators that took place years later) were established in military bases, military schools, police precincts, and "safe" houses, unleashing a reign of terror that replicated quite literally the "Night and fog" policy of the Nazi regime.[4] The mass media were tightly leashed, and the "disappearance" of several journalists reinforced that message of silence. Any voice of concern or opposition was crushed, while the repression continued as a routine much after any resemblance of armed opposition had disappeared.

The standard procedure was for armed police or military groups with police escort to kidnap individuals in their workplaces, or in the street, or, break into their homes usually by night, blindfold the victims, be they individuals or whole families, and drive them away in unmarked cars. Victims would seldom be seen or heard from again. In the course of these abductions, which frequently included ransacking any valuables that could be found, the operatives would tell any witness or family member that mentioning anything about the procedure they witnessed to anybody would seal the fate of the abducted while, if they kept silence, the victims may reappear alive. If, in spite of such threats, family members would attempt to denounce the kidnapping or inquire about the whereabouts of the victim, both the police and the military would deny any knowledge of the matter, suggesting that perhaps those disappeared may have in fact escaped abroad, or may have been kidnapped by a subversive group, while the judicial system would raise their arms and shoulders in a complicitous silence, the Catholic church would remain silent, and the media would refrain from printing or denouncing these events. With very few exceptions, the end of those detained was either death under torture or in a subsequent execution and burial in common unmarked graves or— another frequent method—they were dumped, generally drugged but alive, from military airplanes overflying the ocean (Verbitsky, 1996). They were, in fact, literally made to disappear.[5]

The rationale for such acts, as explained by the military government, was their need to counter the threat posed by urban guerilla groups. "If one out of every ten people we capture belongs to the enemy," stated the then commander-in-chief of the army, "the whole thing becomes worthwhile." A reign of terror, a "culture of fear" (Corradi, Weiss Fagen, & Garreton, 1992) was thus established that gagged any protest. The official control of the mass media, in turn, contributed to the ominous silence around processes that were, at the same time, vox populi.

However, the strong support that the military junta received from the Catholic Church as well as from sectors of landowners and strong industrialists eroded progressively. That was accompanied by the general population's increasingly vocal disaffection with the military junta, a major economic crisis, and the failure of a botched military adventure created to raise popular fervor and support (the Malvinas/Falkland War) that cost the lives of thousands of young men. Humiliated, unpopular, internally plagued by reciprocal accusations of ineptitude, and bombarded by the international public opinion about its repressive methods, the military junta conceded to national elections. As a result, by the end of 1983 a civilian president was constitutionally elected by popular consensus. The new government established an investigative body, the (Argentine) National Commission on the Disappearance of Individuals (CONADEP), which amassed, from the testimony of survivors and witnesses, a gruesome archive of savagery that made possible in the long run the trial, indictment, and imprisonment of some of the perpetrators (CONADEP, 1984).

It is not the intent of this book to present a full account of that horror— there are ample documents for those interested, among which the reports of the above-mentioned CONADEP and of Amnesty International (1975, 1987), and other publications (e.g. Camarasa, Felice, & Gonzalez, 1985; Corradi et al., 1992; Marchak, 1999; and Catoggio, 2010)—but, rather, to provide a sociopolitical frame within which took place the family interview that constitutes the core of this chapter. In this interview the virtual presence of both disappeared and repressors will become palpable.

Context of the Consultation

The interview took place in Buenos Aires early in 1983, in an ambiguous political climate in which the debilitated military regime, still in place, had announced that it would call for general elections later that year—while the public opinion was still doubting whether that event would ever take place.

I should point out that this consultation was not experienced as a "risky activity" by me, the interviewer, or perhaps even by the family, for several reasons. First, the military regime's messianic rhetoric and its repressive apparatus were drastically weakened, the censorship of the mass media was reduced, and there had been no recent instances of political disappearances. Second, having lived abroad for many years, I had been spared the imprinting of extreme precautions, fear, and self-censorship that affected the majority of the Argentine population, a result of the years of their having learned to survive under a mantle of collective political repression. And third, this was a bona fide routine intake consultation conducted in a reputable mental health center.

However, for the small team of professionals that observed this consultation from behind a one-way mirror, this interview became an extremely novel and moving experience: political disappearances and their impact on their family was a subject considered still "too hot to handle," and the open discussion of these issues, as it took place in this interview, was for many of the observers their first *in vivo* exposure to an all-too-familiar event that until then was not discussed beyond the boundaries of conversations among friends in the privacy of their homes, or in the occasional editorials of one maverick newspaper, in itself a new event.

The Family Interview

As mentioned above, this family interview was conducted in the offices of a private family-oriented mental health clinic, which was the main resource for the mental health services of a health insurance company. The family was referred to that clinic by a public school counselor, who was concerned because of the depressed demeanor and avoidance–hostile behavior of their 7-year-old boy. When the person who requested the appointment by phone was informed that the parents of the child were expected to participate in the initial consultation, as was the routine intake procedure of the clinic, she answered hesitantly that both the boy and his 9-year-old sister considered her to be their mother, but she was, in fact, their aunt, and that her brother, considered by the children to be their father, was, in turn, their uncle. The ambiguous message was telling much more: she was informing the receptionist that there were things she could not reveal, at least not by phone, which was considered at that times an "unsafe" medium. The receptionist had little doubt that this family was one in which there were *desaparecidos*, and she wisely rephrased the request: she invited to the initial consultation those family members who live together with the child.

I happened to be in Buenos Aires that week, and engaged that day in providing a day of clinical supervision and consultations for the therapists of that clinic. In that context I was asked to conduct the initial consultation with this family, which was promising to be rather challenging, even more considering the prediction that it would contain such a "hot" issue. The group with whom I was working, namely, the eight therapists from the clinic, would observe the interview from behind a one-way mirror, if the family would accept the setting.[6]

Participants in this first interview were the 7-year-old boy, his 9-year-old sister, their 58-year-old paternal grandmother and her other three offspring, the children's 32-year-old aunt, and their 30- and 24-year-old uncles, the former with a heavy cast on one forearm. According to records, the average education of the adults of this family was completion of high school and their socio-economic insertion placed them in the lower strata of middle class.

I greet them in the waiting room and, while the group is entering the office, the aunt stops me in the corridor, saying in low voice, "Doctor, I would like to speak with you separately." "Please, come in, let's talk inside, madam," I answer. She insists, "But it is because of the kids." I respond in a supportive tone, "Ma'am, whatever family secrets there may be, kids generally <u>know</u>. However, you are welcome not to say anything that you believe should not be said in front of them and to stop me if you believe that I am doing that."

I maintained that stance because, in most cases, in fact "kids know," that is, most family secrets reflect a shared agreement of *all participants* that certain issues should not be mentioned. I also believe that most efforts "to protect the children" are undertaken to protect the adults (e.g., most couples who do not separate "because of the children" have a hard time confronting the pains and tribulations of separating regardless of the effects on the children). I also wanted to protect myself from a potential triangulation—a privileged contact with one leaving others out of the conversation.

We enter the room and the family sits in the following order (clockwise): grandmother, sister, aunt, uncle with cast, boy, and younger uncle. I take the remaining chair between younger uncle and grandmother. As we are seating, the sister points out and comments with animation and surprise "Look, grandma! Look at the microphones!"

This comment expresses, in all likelihood, the whole family's alertness and mistrust, potentiated by the country's political climate and their own circumstances. Therefore, I respond accordingly.

I clarify again the team approach of the clinic, remind them that, as they had been informed when their appointment was confirmed, I was going to see them only for this first consultation and that several colleagues, including the therapist that would continue working with them, would be observing us behind the one-way mirror. I invite them to visit the observation room at that moment or at any time "to see how it looks and who is there." They politely decline the offer but seem more relaxed.

I ask, "Who made the phone call?" Aunt answers that she did. I invite her to explain the reason for the consultation. She states, "The problem is that both kids, who are my nephew and my niece, have problems at school and look very depressed, especially the boy. But the problem is really that my little brother is getting married." I ask, "Who is the little brother?" Younger uncle says with a slightly embarrassed voice, "I am." Everybody laughs lightly. I ask "little brother" what is his age, and he answers, "Twenty-four." Aunt comments, "The children call him 'daddy', and call me 'mommy.'"

As if in passing, aunt offers me a crucial piece of information, namely, that she and her brother are raising these children. This comment, in that political climate, further confirms that the children's parents have been "disappeared" and hence the aunt's "secret." I indicate that I registered the explicit information ("Do you have any other title . . . ?", see below) but decide not to pursue its implications immediately. I weave my interview around the family story for a while rather than focusing on the family secret, as dramatic events operate as "powerful attractors" that tend to reduce the flexibility of the conversation. In addition, "talking around" hidden themes is context-appropriate: I replicate and respect, at least in the initial moments of the interview, the way that subject is treated both by the family and by the public in general, if/when mentioned at all.

I ask the older uncle—the one with the cast—what is his role in the family. He replies candidly "I'm just an uncle." "Do you have any other title in addition to 'uncle'?" "Well, I'm also the kids' godfather." He clarifies that he is home infrequently because of his occupation as a merchant sailor, but he had broke his forearm in a job-related accident and had to remain ashore as he needed surgery and subsequent rehabilitation procedures for several months. To complete the circle of grownups, I ask grandmother, "And who are you in the family?" She replies that she is the grandmother. "Are there any other immediate family members?", I inquire, and they respond negatively. I ask grandmother, "And your husband?" "He died not long ago. But we have been separated already many years ago, and he wasn't really a member of the family."

Returning to the reason for the consultation, aunt/mommy comments that uncle/daddy is planning to get married in two years and "already the problems are starting." She adds, "The kid is very worried. He told me a few days ago that when daddy gets married he will no longer have a dad, because if and when daddy has kids of his own, 'they won't let me call him daddy'." I ask uncle/daddy, "When you have children, how are you going to feel about all this?" He answers, "Well, by then the kid is going to be a bit older and he will understand." I ask him, "What is it that he has to understand?" "That I am really his uncle." "And that therefore he should call you 'uncle'?" "No, he may call me 'daddy' if he wants, but he should understand that I am his uncle." I ask the boy, "Now do you understand that he is your uncle?" The boy answers a straight "Yes." Uncle/daddy comments, "He says 'yes' but he really feels 'no'." Aunt comments, "He is so attached to his daddy that at night he generally doesn't want to go to sleep until daddy arrives." Grandmother adds, "And his daddy also favors him too much." Aunt continues, "He worries me because I see him crying. The other day the kid told me secretly that he had confided his fears to daddy and daddy reassured him telling him that he wasn't going to get married." The boy mumbles a disclaimer, and aunt tells him, "One has to tell all the truth to the doctor." At that moment I tell her, "You are right. Which brings me to another issue: What was the secret that you wanted to talk about while we were coming in?"

The moment for this question was chosen not only to piggyback on the aunt's own moral stance about truthfulness, but also because I sensed that by then the family had relaxed and had signaled a certain level of comfort and trust. (I should add that, if she would have refused to answer, or to do it marginally, I would not have insisted or returned to the issue during the rest of the interview but waited and to see whether it would emerge without further pressure.)

Aunt replies, "Well, the kids don't know exactly why their parents aren't with them."

This behavior of talking about children in the third person in the children's presence, as if they weren't there is a fairly frequent behavior in our society. However, that doesn't make it a less amazing a practice, especially when children are as lucid and tuned-in as these two seemed to be. However, my goal in this interview—or in any other one, as will also be commented on in the interview with the Moroccan/Belgian family in Chapter 5—was not to "correct their style" but at the most to model alternatives, challenging family myths and their code of silence. Thus, I chose to maintain this group's semantic style while progressively undermining it by actively including the children at different times as responsible actors.

I state, "Allow me to ask a complex question: What difference would their knowing or not knowing make to your current circumstances? Because, if I understand the situation correctly, for all practical purposes their biological parents are dead. Or aren't they?" They all look stunned. Aunt/mommy mumbles in a correcting tone, "They . . . left." I ask again, always with an empathetic tone of voice, "I am fully aware that this is a very hard question, but, for all practical purposes, are they dead or alive?" After a brief silence, aunt/mommy answers, in a tone between doubtful and didactic, as if talking to a child, "They are alive, somewhere." "Where?" "Somewhere." "Have any of you had any contact with them?" She answers softly, "No." "Have any of you had any contact with them whatsoever since they disappeared already, what, several years ago?"

In the middle of this conversation, I introduce the word "disappeared," fully aware of the fact that it was not just a verb. In that country and context it was also a noun for people kidnapped, and presumably killed by government agents for political reasons.

Aunt/mommy answers, "No." "So, what you have is the hope that they be alive." "Yes," she answers. I ask uncle/daddy, "What is your own intuition in this regard?" "That they are alive." I ask grandmother and she answers, as if stating the obvious, "They are dead, doctor." I ask the same question to the older uncle and he also states with an unambiguous tone of voice, "They are dead." Noting that the girl is squirming in her chair as if anxious to talk, I ask her, "What is your own intuition?" She answers, "For me they aren't," while the boy shrugs his shoulders signaling "I don't know."

I should note that this macabre poll did not begin by design, but evolved in the flow of the conversation, and was carried on in a soft, quite tender tone of voice. However, it had a powerful effect of shattering both the silenced subject and any pretense of consensus in the family in that regard.

Uncle/daddy adds, as footnoting the girl's comment, "She saw it all." I ask the girl, "Oh, what is it that you saw?" She says, "I was very little. I was, I believe, three years old. The four of us were living with another aunt, my mom's sister. Once, two men came in the middle of the night and began to bang at the door. My aunt said 'Let's open the door and see what happens.' And there were these two men with machine guns and others at the door. My aunt grabbed me, saying, 'You come with me to the corridor,' and the men talked with mom and dad." Grandmother corrects her, "Your dad wasn't there." The child says, "Oh, yes, he ran after the car afterwards!" Grandmother comments to me, "That part is not true," and to the granddaughter, "But go on." The girl continues, "I escaped from my aunt and went to the kitchen with mom. They were asking her for her name and those things, and told her, 'You must come with us.' And they took her to their car. It was about midnight. I then saw my dad leaving the kitchen and running after their car." Uncle states, "She is mixing truth and fantasy, because most of it is as it happened but her father wasn't there. As far as we know, the father was picked up at work. We don't even know for sure." I state, "I have the impression that it is not only the kids, but also the grownups who are combining facts and hopes." I then ask aunt/mommy and uncle/daddy—the two who said that the disappeared couple were alive—"In addition to your hopes, do you have any hint whatsoever that may indicate that they may be alive?" "No, nothing whatsoever, just intuition," answers aunt/mommy on behalf of both. I state, "I will ask you a question that sounds a bit awkward, but I can't find any other way of putting it: What is the use of having this belief?" Aunt/mommy answers, "It is in order to keep my brother alive," and uncle/daddy agrees, adding, "In order to keep hope." "So you two carry a terrible responsibility," I tell them, "Your mom and your older brother believe that they are dead. If you would join them in their belief, if you would lose

(continued)

(continued)

your faith, then they would die." The aunt agrees, "Yes, if I wouldn't believe or something." I continue: "You keep them alive with your hope. What a heavy load! And you don't have too many allies in this matter." Uncle/daddy adds, "And I am afraid of how the kids would react to that information, not when they are grownups, but now." (A strange formulation, considering the active role of the children in this conversation!) I turn to the boy, "So your sadness may be related not only to the possibility that he [uncle/daddy] may be leaving you as daddy, but to all the death and void that exist in the family." And, addressing the rest of the group, "So what he is expressing may be the sadness of the whole family." This comment is followed by a pensive silence.

The silence, without any visible emotional echo (and dissonant with my own emotions at that moment), made me think that I was moving too quickly, beyond their own pace. So I return to the prior theme.

I ask aunt/mommy, "Where could they be if they were alive?" "Well, I don't know. Perhaps out of the country, or in an undisclosed concentration camp, or crazed by torture and having lost their senses and their memory." In response to her vague tone of voice and gestures, I comment tenderly, "In fact, I have the impression that you yourself sense that your theory doesn't hold much water." They all agree. I comment to grandmother that it must be very difficult and painful to talk about the subject. Grandmother and uncle/ daddy answer in a duet that the situation is indeed very different from, for instance, death by disease, because in their circumstances there is a slight possibility that they may not have died. If they reappear, adds uncle/daddy, the kids would accuse the family of lying. However, if the kids were told that their parents are alive but they end up not reappearing, the kids would believe that their parents have abandoned them. I summarize, "The family's agreement is, then, that the biological parents of the two kids are probably, but not certainly, dead." All of them (children included!) agree with my formulation. I continue, "The most difficult thing to tolerate is the lack of total certainty."

Having talked about the unspeakable, it is time to deal with the impact of those terrible circumstances on their present reality.

I continue, "However, for all practical purposes, they are dead, and you [aunt/ mommy] are the mother and you [uncle/daddy] are the father of the children. For five or six years now you have fulfilled at all times the 'mother' and 'father' roles and functions, isn't it true? Has there been any other person who has fulfilled the 'mother' function and the 'father' function for the kids?" "No," they respond, mesmerized by a more sacramental tone in my voice and the slower, almost ceremonial pace of this exchange. I state, "So, independently of any other event, it should be acknowledged that you [aunt/mommy] have the title of 'honorary mother' and you [uncle/daddy] the title of 'honorary father' and nobody can claim it away from you."

While I make this statement, I stand up and ceremonially perform a gesture of pinning an award or medal on the lapel of each of them. Almost in a trance-like state, all of them follow my movements and even look at their "decorated" chests. It is an intense, solemn moment.

I continue, "Forty years from now, both of you kids can keep on calling them 'mommy' and 'daddy', because you two [aunt/mommy and uncle/daddy] have the badges of 'honorary mother' and 'honorary father'." A silence, filled with intense emotion, ensues.

This powerful ritual was pivotal, as it left us all in a sort of trance, in the confluence between drama and the sacred. In fact, the afterglow of that ceremony noticeably tinted the rest of the interview.

Shifting to a more empathic, less solemn tone, I tell the boy, "But I see that you are stuck in a difficult situation, because any kids that your daddy may have after he marries will be tough competition." The boy answers, as if trying to convince me, "Yes, but he could explain to them what happened, and that I have been calling him 'dad' before and that I could keep on calling him 'dad' then." I respond, "That may sound reasonable, but it really depends on whether your daddy agrees or not." And, to the uncle/daddy, "I am asking you, as holder of the title of 'honorary father': Do you foresee abandoning that title in the future?" He answers, "No, and he knows that." I state, "Well, he seems to be requesting from you certain guarantees. I should add that it is a

(continued)

(continued)

request that honors you, as not too many people have fulfilled so thoroughly the title of 'honorary father.'" Uncle/daddy tells the boy, "You can always, always call me 'daddy', and you should know that." The boy looks at him with intensity while I tell the boy "As daddy has the title of 'honorary father,' you in turn have the title of 'honorary son,' which guarantees you a bond for life." They all assent gravely while I "pin a medal" on the boy's lapel. A short silence ensues.

It could be argued that in the preceding dialogue I am, so to speak, twisting uncle/daddy's arm. However, this was a logical consequence of the awards ritual, and the dialogue took place in a conversational, low-tension manner and evolved in a non-coercive way. In order to increase the impact of this agreement, after these exchanges I maintained a silence for about 10 seconds, and then shifted subjects. In the subsequent sequence, my choice of subject was guided by my belief in the frequent correlation between enmeshment in families—regardless of how context-appropriate that enmeshment may be—and psychosomatic manifestations under stress. Perhaps I was also reacting to the massive cast on the uncle's arm.

After the silence I turn to grandmother, "Ma'am, I would like to have your perspective on something. How has been the health of this family, as you see it?" This question triggers a collective roar of laughter. Grandmother states, "During these last two years it has been a major disaster, doctor, just an interminable series of things! First, my former husband got cancer. Then my gall bladder acted up. Then my husband got sicker and died. Then came the accident of the kid [referring to the sailor], with his arm almost destroyed, in a cast for a year, graft surgery, and all that. Then, after his accident, I had a gastric hemorrhage due to an old ulcer reactivated by medication I was taking for my arthritis, and I was in bad shape. And also the little one [referring to uncle/daddy] has a swollen ganglion that has to be biopsied in order to find out what's going on. Summarizing, health is a big disaster. And my daughter, with all her worries about the kids, everything she eats upsets her stomach." Uncle adds, "We all have ulcers in this family. I also have an ulcer in the duodenum." I comment, "So, you are a family of worriers." The girl adds jovially, "And we kids have indigestion and colitis." Grandmother concludes, "Since two years ago we haven't had any respite."

Once the correlation between physical symptoms and emotions is proposed and accepted, it seemed reasonable to anchor this description by establishing a correlation between emotions and events.

*I ask grandmother, "Does your ulcer have to do with your husband's death?"
She answers, "No, it has to do mainly with the children. They are at an age
in which, understandably, they are sort of rowdy, but my age doesn't tolerate that. I get very tense, and I close myself behind doors or I start to shout."
I ask, "Does this method work for you?" Grandmother answers, "Sometimes
it does, because the kids shut up when they see me very upset. But by then
I am already in a bad mood, which is really what I should try to avoid." I
state, "If I understand correctly, to be nervous and to have ulcers is a kind of
family style, and as such it must be very difficult to change. When did your
ulcer start?" "Six years ago. Then it healed by itself, but this medication for
my low-back pain reopened it." "So, in fact, your ulcer started with the terrible situation of the disappearance of your son and daughter-in-law." "Yes,
much nerves, too much nerves." I ask aunt, "Since when have you had your
ulcer?" "Since two years ago." "Do you relate it to something in particular?"
"No, as far as I can remember I have always been very nervous." I comment,
"Here, quite the contrary, you look very calm and collected." She states,
"Yes, but I take pills for that." Uncle adds, "She takes pills for everything!"
At that moment, in an apparent non sequitur, the girl tells an episode in
which uncle/daddy, returning from work late at night, heard a lugubrious
voice calling him by name from a house under construction, and he became
so scared of the "ghost" that he ran all the way home, several blocks away,
arriving pale and exhausted. Everybody laughs while aunt praises the girl's
exceptional memory.*

Tempted as I was to tie with a comment the themes of the "ghost," the fear, the police state, and the disappeared (and worried that I would reopen a discussion about who believes what), I choose to stick to the association between the physical symptoms and the chronic stress in the family, an area that I considered of concern in this family.

*I tell the uncle/sailor, "I have the impression that the only really accidental
event seems to have been the one you had with your arm. (And turning
to uncle/daddy.) But perhaps another experience that was felt as a serious
accident by the family may have been your own engagement. When did you*

(continued)

(continued)

announce it to the family?" "Two years ago." "Not surprising," I respond, with a humorous tone. Uncle/daddy, establishing the correspondence of dates between that announcement and the beginning of his sister's and his mother's (other) symptoms, comments, only half in jest, "I hope it is not all my fault." I answer, "Well, at least it underlines the importance of your role and presence for the whole family. In fact, all this abundance of symptoms may show how viscerally important you all are for one another. There are also good indicators that there are painful and scary ghosts that must be visited."

Rich as this fragment of the interview may be, it is also rather self-explanatory. Chronologies can be traced while maintaining a conversational mode, symptoms can be used as metaphors or somatic counterparts of emotions, and the almost surreal nature of the events of this family makes "magical" or "fantastic realism," ghosts and all, a reasonable style.

At this moment, I begin to wrap up the interview, proposing a synthesis that, in a context of positive connotation, justifies the consultation because of their collective overload, rather than due to the original reason for consultation—the boy's symptoms—thus de-centering him from the role of "identified patient."

I comment, "You are a family in which everybody is enormously responsible, almost as if competing about who is going to be able to handle more loads. You [grandmother] seem like Atlas, carrying the whole world on your shoulders, until your back hurts. You [aunt/mommy] are so concerned about taking care of everybody in the family that you don't have time to take care of yourself. And you [uncle/daddy], with your own personal life project intertwined with the life of the whole family and with your position as honorary father . . ." Grandmother interjects with pride, "I don't believe that there are many other brothers and sisters that would have taken the enormous responsibility they have assumed with such dedication. You cannot imagine it. It is excessive!" I tell grandmother, "I wonder who they learned this excessive virtue from!" Everybody laughs. Uncle adds, "You should not forget that our dad was a sailor and he wasn't at home most of the time. Our mother accomplished in fact the double function of mother and father for all of us."

The interview is near closure. The remaining priority is to establish continuity between this and subsequent interviews.

> *I state, "What I find also admirable is that, being hyper-responsible as you are as a family, you all have been able to decide not to increase the load of taking care of everything and, instead, you have chosen to seek help from trusted people from the outside." Uncle comments, "One of the problems with the kids is that they are so bright that if we want to avoid answering their questions they won't let us, in spite of our being sometimes incapable ourselves of answering those questions." I answer, "It must be a challenge to be grandmother and uncle and honorary mother and honorary father of kids who are bright, and who ask many important questions." And, to the children, "But, in fact, with your questions you are helping the family very much with issues that are difficult to talk about but important to clear up."*

The interview is coming to an end. I invite into the room and introduce to the family the colleague from the Clinic staff who had been assigned to continue working with them, and that until then was part of the group of professionals that had observed the interview through the one-way screen. She greets them, they exchange social graces, and she schedules the next appointment with the family. I shake hands with everybody, and grandmother hugs me—a gesture that is not culturally expected and is a clear indication of appreciation. As they leave the office, the therapist invites them again to visit the observation room, which they accept. They are introduced collectively to the handful of colleagues who were observing the interview—some of them still wiping their tears—and they all exchange social pleasantries. The family then leaves, while I remain with the group commenting on our views of the interview, venting emotions, and discussing politics.

In fact, most of the small group of colleagues who observed the consultation behind the one-way mirror had been openly crying during parts of the consultation, and some had to leave the observation room occasionally in an attempt to control the intensity of their own emotions. They ended up expressing their appreciation for the way the session had been conducted—and exhausted with the experience. It was, one of them said, as if they had entered a forbidden, dangerous territory, and recovered by that token a true dimension of their responsibility as therapists, and as human beings. In turn, the interview also entailed for me an extremely intense emotional experience. I felt elated and extremely fortunate for having been able to be there for this family at that time. I admired the family's capacity for endurance and survival as well as the strengths, openness, and courage with which they embraced change. And I was also relieved by my impression that I had succeeded in facilitating the beginning of a transformative process.

Subsequent Sessions

This family was seen in therapy a total of seven additional interviews, scheduled three to seven weeks apart.[7]

In the first follow-up session, the family informs the therapist that the girl is crying more, appears to be angry all the time, and is engaging in frequent confrontations with her brother and with the grownups. Following an empathetic statement by the therapist, the child sobs inconsolably, "They called me damned. Two girls at school called me damned." The therapist elicits the fact that the girl doesn't talk with anybody, including family members, about any painful experience. Grandmother comments that when "all that" happened and the kids came to live with them, they were told that they shouldn't tell anything to anybody. The therapist comments that the girl understood that instruction to the extreme, and has maintained it faithfully for all these years, bottling up her emotions as if that would keep her parents alive. She supports the girl without recommending any change. The boy, in turn, states that he and his sister want to have a pet, but they (the adults) don't allowed them to. He comments about a puppy dog that they found wounded in the street and which they had brought home and loved very much, kept him while he was healing, but which had then escaped. As the therapist was trying to make up her mind whether to associate this to the disappeared parents or to the fear of abandonment of the children—resonating with the theme of the first consultation—to her surprise the adults in the family, who had remained rather silent during the first part of the session, begin to discuss with animation the pros and cons of having a pet in their apartment. The therapist facilitates the discussion without taking sides.

The second follow-up session is focused on their individual and collective daily routines. It becomes clear that each family member carries on his or her activities—study or work—while maintaining a staunch social isolation. The family lives in an apartment on a commercial street, rather than in a family-oriented neighborhood; both kids attend a school located near aunt/mommy's workplace, some 20 miles from their home, which precludes after-school contact with their school companions; when the girl goes to Catholic Sunday School or shopping, she is always escorted by aunt/mommy, who also takes her to and from school; at school the girl stays inside the classroom during recess, doing homework or helping other kids with theirs; the boy, who appears either distracted or misbehaving in class, is frequently punished by the teacher by expelling him from the classroom, and spends time playing by himself in the school corridors; during weekends, aunt, who works late hours, sleeps most of the time, grandmother stays by herself or goes out alone, and uncle/daddy occasionally takes the children to the park to play. Otherwise, the children spend their weekend playing by themselves or watching television in the apartment. The therapist connotes positively the mischievousness of the boy: he is intelligent and ingenious and, as he gets bored in class, he uses the school as his amusement park. This leads to a family exchange about the need for them to develop more child-oriented activities, and they agree among themselves to find a soccer club for the boy as well as allow the girl to walk with a neighbor's daughter to the nearby Sunday school, as she had requested. The therapist assumes strategically a "restraining" stance: letting the kids go a bit will be hard for all the grownups, that is, "normalizing" the family situation will be accompanied by sadness, as it implies abandoning hope for the re-appearance of the disappeared; because of their tendency to respond to stress with bodily ailments, she advised, they should proceed slowly, exploring their own tolerance for the change.

The third follow-up session finds the family enthusiastic. The boy has joined a soccer club and the girl has begun to go to Sunday school with a friend, with whom she also has registered to become a girl scout. Issues of authority emerge as grandmother complains that aunt/mommy and uncle/daddy are too permissive. The therapist includes the more marginalized uncle/sailor "as a consultant" in this discussion in order to promote his involvement with the children.

During the fourth follow-up session the family members comment that they did not find themselves sad, as predicted by the therapist two sessions before, but, rather, confused because of the new range of social situations they are confronting. For instance, they are organizing a birthday party for the girl, to which, for the first time, they are inviting non-family guests such as friends of the children and a neighbor. But, aunt comments with concern, these people may not understand why "daddy" is there with his fiancée. The girl comments with some distress, "But I don't want to tell them that they are *like* parents for me but that they are really my aunt and uncle." The therapist praises as a collective achievement how openly the girl is now able to express her feelings with the family, and also "normalizes" the collective confusion as an unavoidable and understandable effect of this period of transition. Grandmother states that, in spite of having a number of friends, she also cannot talk about her disappeared son and daughter-in-law, not unlike the girl. Grandmother and granddaughter chit chat about it and smile at each other understandingly.

The fifth follow-up session takes place after a democratic government has been elected, and the population has been exposed to a flood of reports on the disappeared through the news media. The family discusses this theme openly and agrees that, in all likelihood, the kids' parents are dead, while hoping without too much hope that they may reappear. The boy says, "If my mother and father come to pick me up, I will not go with them. I will stay with mommy and daddy, as I love them and I don't love the others." And the girl states somewhat didactically, "If they come to fetch us, we have to live all together in the same house, them, grandma, our uncles and aunts, and all of us." Evaluating the goals of therapy, the family states that the problems with the children are subsiding, and that they had finished their elementary school year more than successfully. They also report with some admiration and surprise that the girl has been able to speak with two friends about their aunt and uncle "who are for all practical purposes her parents," and about the parents whose whereabouts are unknown. Aunt in turn comments that she has started additional studies in a community college. Furthermore, nobody has been sick in the family for over six months, which is defined jokingly as deserving an entry in the *Guinness Book of Records*. The therapist, in jest, recommends a minor relapse "to avert the evil eye." The family members propose to discontinue scheduled sessions. The therapist agrees to this, while informing them that she will be available if needed.

A month later, they request a sixth session, to which only the adults in the family attend in order to discuss a conflict between the grandmother and her offspring. Grandmother wishes to add the name of her son and daughter-in-law to the list of disappeared opened up by the newly created (Argentine) National Commission on the Disappearance of People, and to provide all the information they have about the procedure during their kidnapping. To her surprise, her three offspring have openly disagreed, wanting "to leave things the way they are, and not make this case public." The older uncle argues that he is afraid of being singled out as a member of a possibly subversive family and that may blacklist him for jobs as a merchant sailor. Aunt is afraid that it would generate mistrust among her co-workers, as until then she had never mentioned anything to anybody at the office where she works about the matter. In addition, both uncles/parents voice skepticism about the commitment of the new civilian government on the matter: "They won't do anything. They are all alike." Grandmother expresses her need for their support and says that she cannot do it all alone. The therapist suggests that, while the kids and the grandmother were able to shed the instruction not to talk, the three siblings need a longer lapse of silence because of the heavy weight of the secrets on their souls.

Two months later, grandmother calls and requests a couple of individual sessions. She had undergone emergency bypass surgery a month earlier and is in need of support. In turn, her daughter, in a change of stance, has begun to provide testimony about the disappearance of the children's parents to CONADEP, arguing that her mother should not testify because she is still recovering from surgery. In addition, they had started procedures toward their legal adoption of the children. Themes that the therapist discusses with the grandmother include "irrational" guilt, ambiguous loss, relief, and the strange experience of allowing time to flow again (a theme that I had discussed with the group of therapists after the session and that I will pick up below).

Discussion

For purposes of focusing this discussion, one of the issues that emerged as salient in this interview is the way in which catastrophic loss and living in a repressive regime—and the internalized oppressive instructions that frequently persist for quite a while after the external conditions have changed[8]—affected the communication style, the insertion into their social network and, overall, the worldview of all members of this family. It also illustrates components of a therapeutic process aimed at changing the impact of that climate and of those instructions.

In the same way that the experience of torture leaves indelible marks on the worldview of the tortured (Amnesty International, 1975; Mollica, 1988; Ritterman, 1985), and just as torture itself is an act that mystifies and robs the victim of both dignity and language (Scarry, 1985), the ripple effect of being a member of a family in which another member has disappeared without trace is profound. This drama is compounded by the effects of living in a country where the State, supposedly the defender of the individual's rights, not only violates those rights but also denies and mutes protests about such violation through mystifications, threats, and silence. The family, in fact, is forced to adopt and replicate in its own language and in its social behavior the mystifying and secretive style of the political regime (Droeven & Crescini, 1987; Kohen, 1988; Sluzki, 1994).

During the admission interview, the limbo shrouded by silence where the disappeared inhabit appeared as a conviction tightly held and staunchly defended by members of the family. This constitutes a prime example of the notions of *high boundary ambiguity* and of *ambiguous loss* developed by Paulina Boss (1984, 1988, 2006) in reference to families with a member who, in the words of that author, is "physically absent but psychologically present" or vice versa. The first case fits the experience of many families of American soldiers who were defined as "missing in action" in the course of the Vietnam conflagration, and of families with a disappeared—probably abducted—child: the family tends to keep the disappeared person's belonging intact, their room as it was when they were at home and even their place at the table unoccupied, and their virtual presence is experienced on a daily basis, in a protracted struggle between hope and mourning that may last for years. The second case of *ambiguous loss* corresponds to the description of "physically present but psychologically absent," applied to families with a member in an advanced state of Alzheimer's disease, or in a protracted comma, where the body is still there but the family has, in many cases, already mourned in part their loss, and is struggling between attachment to the shadow of that person and the wish that they finish their process of dying. One way or the other, these situations of high ambiguity lead to a "freezing" of time, severely disrupting any attempt by the family to go on with their life, mourn, and find resilient ways of dealing with the current as well as future stresses, arresting the normative developmental processes in children and in adults.

Throughout the initial interview, the adult members of the family we are discussing used one or another euphemisms ("they are not there," "they left") to refer to the void left by the disappeared family members. In fact, their disappearance seems to be dealt with as if would have been an odd vanishing act rather than the result of human violence. Also, the family expressed both realistic and rather farfetched beliefs about the whereabouts of the disappeared—much as survivors of disasters do when searching for a meaning or explanation, or when they favor seeking whom to blame in a natural, non-preventable catastrophic event within the range of what is generally called "acts of God" (Horowitz, 1985). The disappeared seem to inhabit a no-person's land, a limbo; this has been described as taking place in families of the political disappeared (Droeven & Crescini, 1987; Kohen, 1988), families of missing in action (Boss, 1984; Hunter, 1983), and families of kidnapped or otherwise disappeared children (Boss, 1988; Boss & Greenberg, 1984).

It should be noted that, throughout the interview, the verb "to disappear" was either nominalized (a person is "a disappeared") or used in its passive voice (he/she "was disappeared") in sentences in which the agent of action ("by the military," "by the government") was omitted. This grammatical sleight of hand reconstitutes and perpetuates the repressive environment that had generated it, until the new usage of the term included in its assumed meaning that it is a reference to a political act, unless otherwise qualified. Further, the theme is discussed throughout this interview without any trace of indignation or blame placed on the military operative that led to the kidnappings or on the dictatorial regime. We know from subsequent information that their blaming and their indignation surfaced when the political external circumstances and the high exposure to these issues reduced the sense of danger attached to those emotions, perhaps with the help of the therapeutic work done with the family. In fact, both grandmother and aunt/mommy became actively involved with the human-rights trials that began about eight months later in Argentina.

The question posed during the course of the interview about "the difference between knowing and not knowing" seems to synthesize the core obfuscated distinction for this family: To "not know" represents the success of the efforts of the regime, and "to know" recaptures the family's language, its identity, and its chronology. The stressful nature of that transition may have been compounded in this family by the change in political climate, from repression to increased freedom. Paradoxical as it may appear to be, the advent of democratic governments and practices challenge tightly held family patterns and myths built up during the period of governmental repression and thus unleash a major crisis in many families of the disappeared (Droeven & Crescini, 1987).

The family's whole ecology—as transpired clearly throughout the summary of the follow-up sessions—was organized so as to assure the isolation of the family and thus the maintenance of silence about their drama. This injunction—both the one explicitly made by the captors and the one implicitly present by the overall silence of the media and the reign of terror—severely disrupted the family's prior social network and made it difficult for it to be reactivated or for any new social network to be developed in that period of increased stress and diminished resources, precisely when the need for social support is maximal (Sluzki, 1979, 1992a). Correspondingly, issues of autonomy (such as facilitating experiences of independence by the children) are managed so as to generate family rules that foster dependence and discourage autonomy; this was strikingly apparent in the family's description of its social policies. Even more, taking into account that Latino cultural practices lean toward the "enmeshment" pole of the enmeshment–disengagement continuum proposed by Salvador Minuchin (1974), the extreme closure of the boundaries between the core nuclear family and the rest of their world is remarkable. It should also be noted that this is a frequent trait of families of survivors of natural and human-designed disasters, including the Holocaust (Rose & Garske, 1987, among others).

The family's systemic dilemma between change and retention of its shape— the tension between morphogenesis and morphostasis[9]—appeared in all its intensity during the next normative developmental stage for this family, namely, uncle/daddy's announcement of his intentions to marry. This announcement was made four years in advance of the marriage, a rather unusually protracted lapse in that culture. Under circumstances that test any family's resources for change and adaptation, we witness a display of problematic and symptomatic responses that lead to an interpersonal standstill while the relational impact of those symptoms is denied. The intense psychosomatic displays of this family seem to replace the expression of, and dialogues about, an emotional pain that is as unspeakable as the losses from which it stems.

Overall, it could be proposed that the effects of torture as described by Scarry (1986)—namely, that the truth, and, ultimately, the whole construction of the world of the tortured person are shattered by the torture and cannot be reassembled—reaches and affects by proxy the family of the tortured and of the disappeared. Part of the task of this therapy, as I believe the case example shows, has been to offer missing words back to the family—and in that process to make their reality, however terrible it may be, gently available to them, and to develop with them a blueprint for a world that may evolve as they evolve individually and collectively, rather than remaining frozen in a time-less, future-less, silent grief.

In the case reported here, the therapeutic work helped the family to break away from its silencing practices. It also facilitated a weaving of connection between the "neutral" code of somatic dis-ease and the "illegal" code of words and emotions attached to descriptions, thus liberating the family members from the trap of being able to use only symptoms to express their distress. From that and several other respects, the therapeutic process helped them to recover a practice of freedom.

Notes

1 The systematic kidnapping, torturing, and murdering of real or potential political opponents practiced by the State apparatus accompanied by a total denial of that practice reached epidemic proportions in many countries of Latin America, Africa, Asia, and Eastern Europe. As a reaction, the United Nations fostered in 2002 the creation of the International Criminal Court, an independent tribunal charged with investigating and prosecuting crimes against humanity, which includes systematic political disappearances. In turn, the United Nations General Assembly adopted in 2006 the *International Convention for the Protection of All Persons from Enforced Disappearance*. These measures had only a modest effect in curving those practices by authoritarian governments and by all factions during civil wars and protracted conflicts.

2 Both the need and the inability to clarify (in this case, the fate of the disappeared and who was responsible for it) and the need to respond (i.e., in this case, to obey . . . or else) in a context where contradictory or incompatible messages are conveyed (the mystification of the "behave as if nothing is happening" addressed to the witnesses that something terrible is taking place) are key components of the crazy-making set known as the "double-bind" (Bateson, Jackson, Haley, & Weakland, 1956).

3 In the compliance and simultaneous defiance of the governmental injunctions—it was forbidden to congregate, that is, stand together as a group and to voice protests in public— lay the strength of the famous Madres de Plaza de Mayo as they did not talk but promenaded in silence carrying posters with the portraits of "their" disappeared, walking in large circles around the central monument to that plaza in front of the government house—thus skirting the prohibitions to congregate. They would do it on a daily basis, confronting police harassment and governmental debasing attacks as well as the occasional imprisonment and even disappearance of some of them.

4 The *Nacht und Nebel* ("Night and fog") decree was signed by Hitler in 1941 in an effort to eliminate the local resistance against the German occupation of the Netherlands, Belgium and France. In operations that took place in the middle of the night, during curfew hours, those under suspicion were picked up by the Gestapo and imprisoned, without providing to their families any information about their subsequent whereabouts. Those prisoners were routinely tortured to obtain information about resistance networks. Many died under torture and many others were executed and buried in unmarked graves. Those who survived the torture would end up in the Natzweiler-Struthof concentration camp in Alsace (by then annexed as part of the German territory) or the Gross-Ros camp in Poland, where most of them died of starvation or, later, in the infamous "death marches" as the Allied armies advanced one from the west and the other from the east.

5 The persons who disappeared (8,951 according to 1984 CONADEP official figures, and three times that number according to human rights organizations) included females (30%) and males (70%), with age that goes from children age 10 or less (1.1%); adolescents (11%); young adults (58%); and older adults (29.9%). While occasionally young children were tortured in front of their parents in order to extract confessions from them about alleged connections to underground organizations, the vast majority of the very young ones— an estimated 220 (www.uni.illinois.edu/~dstone/dis_background.html), some of them abducted with their parents but most of them born while their mothers were held in captivity—were given for adoption to families of the military and other collaborators of the dictatorial regime, or sold to childless couples.

6 The family was also informed that initial interviews were routinely videotaped, as long as they authorized it. They did, and upon arrival signed an authorization. Needless to say, some data from this family—as is the case with the various clinical encounters discussed in this book—is distorted so as to preserve the anonymity of the family.

7 I gratefully acknowledge the psychologist Raquel Giordano de Guilligan, who provided this helpful follow-up information about the family.

8 This lingering effect of a prolonged oppressive, violent environment persists even when the source of the oppression has been eliminated and can be seen not only in people exposed to (macro) political oppression but also in victims of spousal or parental violence, and in the population at large, as will be exemplified in the next chapter of this book.

9 Morphostasis "refers to those processes in complex system–environment exchanges that tend to preserve or maintain a system's given form, organization or state. Morphogenesis will refer to those processes which tend to elaborate or change a system's given form, structure or state" (Buckley, 1967, pp. 58–59).

Rekindling the Experience of Freedom: Ghosts of a Dictatorship and Reverberations in a Liberating Process

3

Less than two year after the date of the interview discussed in the Chapter 2, I was invited to deliver a keynote address at the First Annual Congress of the Argentine Federation of Systemic Associations, an event that happened to be scheduled a few months after a qualitatively major transitional period in that country: a civilian, democratically elected president had just assumed office, following six years of ruthless military rule.

I was fully aware of the momentous socio-political junction—the reawakening of democratic institutions and of the recovery of individual freedom after a long period of living under a repressive military regime. On that ground I chose, at the last minute, instead of delivering an address on I don't remember what conceptual issue in the field of family therapy, as was announced in the program, to present a videotape of the initial interview with the family discussed in the previous chapter, namely, the one that had suffered the "disappearance" of two central members.

The Professional and Political Context of the Presentation

Argentina is a country with an unusually large number of therapists: Freudian, Kleinian, Wincottian, Kohutian, and Lacanian psychoanalysts; systemic and cognitive individual, couple, and family therapists over-abound, adept at brief and long-term approaches of all colors and persuasions. Since before WWII, psychoanalysis has become a well-established practice in Buenos Aires, aided by the strong intellectual injection of talented Central European professionals escaping Nazism as well as Spaniards escaping Franco's regime. In fact, Argentina had been, for many years, ranked second in the world in terms of the number of psychoanalysts, a training that was limited, until a couple of decades ago, to physicians. In addition, schools of social psychiatry and schools of psychology, the latter created by the free-access state-based university system in the 1960s, were replicated wildly in the 1980s by the uncontrolled mushrooming of private colleges and universities that graduated thousands upon thousands of psychologists, far exceeding the market's ability to absorb them. In this cultural context, to consult with a mental health practitioner, to be in therapy (and to be a therapist) has been perceived as an acceptable practice by the extended middle class of Argentina's largest cities, with little if any negative connotation entailed.

However, during the dreadful 1975–1982 period of the military dictatorship discussed earlier, to be a therapist became a rather problematic practice. Any of several circumstances could place a therapist under jeopardy: (a) patients may end up being subjects of a random or targeted abduction and disappearance, and their therapist's name may appear in their address book or, equally possible, be mentioned and implicated in a fabricated plot during torture; (b) a therapist may be denounced by a disgruntled, overzealous or paranoid neighbor, arguing "suspicious activities" due to the traffic of people they noted in that office, especially if the professional was practicing group therapy; (c) there was an added risk if the therapist was professionally active in a public mental health service or a professional association considered by the military establishment as suspicious because of its rhetoric of commitment to the public sector; and (d) psychotherapy, being in itself a reflective practice, was vaguely considered a subversive practice dangerously contrasting the dominant authoritarian ideology. It should also be noted that the military in charge displayed a clear anti-intellectual and hence anti-therapists bias: the therapeutic sector—mainly represented by psychoanalytically oriented therapies—was seen, probably correctly, as more agnostic (in contrast to the strong Catholic affiliation of the military), more liberal (in contrast to the extreme conservativeness of the military junta and of their internal allies), and more socially concerned than desirable (as an expression of a democratic vocation). The fact that there was a comparatively high proportion of Jews among psychoanalysts didn't help, given the basically anti-Semitic worldview of the Argentine military and conservative class. So, even though it could not be said that therapists in Argentina were core targets of the repressive apparatus, they were nonetheless considered a moderately suspicious group.

During that period of dictatorship, many psychoanalysts, social psychiatrists, and psychologists left the country, some as a safety precaution for themselves and their family, many after being informed that they were on an abduction list or after having experienced hairy near misses with military abduction groups, some, in fact, after having survived torture and being released due to pressure of Amnesty International or an international professional organization. Most therapists, however, remained in the country during the seven years of that *de facto* regime. Those who stayed tended to develop "safer" practices: many simply discontinued all group therapy activities (some kept them for a while but using ad hoc practices such as requesting that group therapy patients enter and leave their office staggered in 5 minute intervals), some screened their patients to select only those who they deemed "safe," that is, patients who did not belong to any ideologically "dangerous" group that may imply a higher risk of disappearance. Many discontinued their involvement with the public sector and some simply ceased practicing as therapists, while, alas, some continued their "business as usual" and took the risk. A small minority, it should be added, developed a committed or militant practice that, with eyes wide open, included working with risky populations, such as families of the *desaparecidos*.

In turn, as part of the general population, to live under this repressive regime entailed avoiding or minimizing some social practices considered potentially dangerous, such as talking about social or political themes in public settings or by phone or with non-intimates. Even further, almost unavoidably, this interdiction to talk became partly, if not totally, internalized as a progressive ban on mentation/perception related to those risky themes: it was better not only to not talk about those issues but also to not think about them and to not perceive them as relevant. "Reality" was, hence, for many, fraught with blind areas.[1] Disappearances, for instance, became, for a sizeable segment of the population—some therapists included—either a fabrication of the discontent or an exaggeration of the Madres de Plaza de Mayo, or one of those nuisances of life that happen to people far away from us and "probably for some (good) reason."

The family therapy convention where this material was presented took place, as mentioned above, as the lid of the repressive apparatus was being lifted, the newly democratically elected government was assuming its responsibilities, and the media was beginning to re-legitimize practices of freedom, including a more open discourse on the *desaparecidos*. However, it should be noted that that convention—neither in the announcements nor in its title—had been explicitly defined as a taking place in a pivotal moment (it had been publicized—albeit, before that momentous political transition—just as "a congress" and not, for instance, as "a celebration of the return of democracy"): Argentina was only slowly awakening, beginning to open its eyes, reactivating its cognition, reconnecting with its emotions almost without knowing, after the long and terrible night of political terror.[2]

The Presentation

After expressing my appreciation for the invitation to address the congress, I started my presentation by defining myself as privileged by the circumstances: while living abroad robbed me from sharing their actual living experience, visiting the country as a professional offered me some unusual glimpses into its realities. I then informed them that, instead of the announced topic for my presentation, I was going to project and discuss the videotape of a consultation that I had conducted less than two years before, and provided the context for that interview. I then projected the actual video of the family interview detailed in Chapter 2 on a large screen, in turn followed by comments and by discussion with the audience.[3]

During the presentation, I paused the videotape at a few key points to clarify interactions that were not clearly audible in the videotape, as well as to introduce comment on some components of the therapeutic processes. That modality of presentation had a certain "cooling," distancing effect, as those short breaks from the continuity of the interview returned the audience to the here-and-now of the congress. I had been tempted beforehand to show the interview without interruptions, especially considering the powerful nature of its central theme. However, I decided otherwise, as I wanted to neutralize the "fascination for content" that powerful themes tend to evoke which, rather than enhancing the audience's capacity to bridge emotions with cognition, may have dissolved it into an overwhelming flood of emotional empathy. In other words, I thought at that time that it was more useful to, so to speak, wake up the audience occasionally from the dream (or nightmare) of that consultation and context.[4]

Once the projection of the interview was concluded, I wrapped up my presentation with a rather succinct and, I would confess, emotional statement about the enactment of freedom embedded in being able to show that session in public without fear of being repressed by the machine of a fascist state. I also commented on the joy of sharing with the audience an experience that I hoped would be emblematic of the new era for that country.

The Reaction of the Audience

The participants to the convention responded to the end of my presentation with an unusually prolonged and enthusiastic applause. The question-and-answer period that followed contained effusive expression of appreciation as well as a number of personal, moving testimonials and statements. When the scheduling need of the convention forced an end to that period of discussion, many vivid exchanges continued in the corridors, as participants surrounded me with comments, confessions, confidences, as well as further accolades, and many other small spontaneous groups remained discussing their impressions and reactions. In subsequent months I also received letters from colleagues who had attended that presentation with appreciative comments and discussing their reactions to it. The comments that follow stem from those exchanges.

Many participants praised my presentation, labeling it as "extremely courageous." I questioned that. Even though I would describe it as very well timed, I argued, I did not experience nor would I define my presentation as an act of courage: the interview proper took place, as already mentioned, during a period in which the repressive activities of the regime had diminished drastically, it had been conducted in a rather safe environment, and—it was worth reminding ourselves—the congress presentation was taking place in the context of an incipient democratic regime. The fact that it was perceived as courageous showed the pervasive load of the effect of repressive regimes, as my presentation had been contextualized according to past, rather than present, risks. In fact, from this angle, it can be asserted that the experience of being an audience to that presentation contributed for many to shake up, and defreeze time, as I will discuss further below.

Among the audience there were some who described a first reaction of fear ("Carlos is crazy!" they thought, "He is placing us all at risk!" "He doesn't understand how things are in Argentina!"). They were actually terrified, convinced, as they later commented, that the police would raid the place and detain us all. They started to scan the auditorium to locate the emergency exits; they were even tempted to leave the room surreptitiously; they were looking around to see whether other colleagues were leaving the auditorium as a barometer to evaluate degrees of danger. And only after a while, slowly in some cases and rather abruptly in others, they became aware that their fears were not founded, that it was no longer dangerous to discuss in public previously forbidden issues such as this one. Their relief and joy was immense.

Many others were, however, simply stunned. As they told me by letter and in conversations in subsequent years, they found themselves unable to move beyond their own emotional reaction, frozen in surprise, or grief, or numbness.[5] The issues and the emotions brought forth by the interview kept on appearing in their mind unexpectedly in the following months, almost as a post-traumatic intrusive recall. It took them a while, they told me, to be able to follow the plea I made at the end of my presentation: "Keep on talking about all this among you and with your patients, keep on talking"—a pragmatic vaccination inspired by the well-known dictum by George Santayana "Those who cannot remember the past are condemned to repeat it."

Some, they told me afterwards, were flooded with shame[6] because of what they described as their prior lack of involvement either due to fear, their not having wanted to believe, or their having defined all those horrors as none of their business. Many wanted to do something about it, to repair as therapists what they felt was a social debt. Therapists to the end, they talked spontaneously about their own "survivor's guilt." Many shifted throughout the presentation from guilt to rage, as they began to experience having been brainwashed by the perverse pervasive practices of the prior repressive government, evidence of their own second-hand victimization. A number of them established conversations, in the very corridor of the auditorium or in the days that followed, with several therapists whom I had identified during my discussion, or had identified themselves during the question-and-answer period, as already working with families of the disappeared, or connected with the Madres de Plaza de Mayo or with the newly formed National Commission for the Investigation of Disappeared Persons, and asked how to become involved themselves.

Others described being progressively flooded with longing reminiscences of people whom they knew and who had either disappeared or left the country in the past few years. They seem to have disconnected at times from the content of my presentation to connect with those powerful reactivated (if not recovered) memories, emerging in many cases with an intensity that surprised them.

Some participants commented later to me that they had been actively involved in working with families of the disappeared, but they had been doing it still semi-secretly, not talking about it outside of their own team, not writing about it or discussing their work publicly, as if it would still be a dangerous activity. Their witnessing my presentation had been an experience that made them realize the importance of discussing those practices openly and publicly, and that their relative secrecy was still a remnant of their recent collective dark past.

Finally, there were participants who were already active and public in their work with human rights and with the families of the *desaparecidos*. They felt validated not only by my presentation but also by the many colleagues who in turn surrounded them requesting additional information, or who contacted them later asking them to join them in their efforts.

Discussion

The repressive apparatus of totalitarian regimes contains in its design two seemingly incompatible goals: to suppress the witness and to inform others of that suppression. A prime and terrible example of the suppression of the witness has been components of the Holocaust killing machine in Auschwitz-Birgenau and other extermination camps, a process aimed at eliminating all witnesses of the very process to which they were subject (a systematic killing and disposing of the bodies of all subjects and then the killing of those who were in charge of disposing of the bodies in the crematories, crowned with a final "housekeeping" frenzy aimed at killing the few remaining prisoners when the liberation armies were near).[7] Another prime example has been the events that serve as political context for this chapter, the Argentine "dirty war," in which thousands of subjects were detained and tortured, and most of them killed, their bodies disposed of without trace. To increase the goal of suppression, those events and procedures avoided outside witnessing. In the case of the Holocaust, Jews (and Gypsies, homosexuals, Jehovah's Witnesses, psychiatric patients, Communists and countless other subgroups) were taken to "detention," "internment," "working," or "transition" (not "extermination") camps, and their neighbors or other occasional "outside" witnesses were informed that those people were being relocated or sent to work camps ("*Arbeit macht frei*"—"Work sets you free"— was written in forged iron letters at the entrance gate to the concentration camps of Auschwitz). In fact, the killing machinery was operating *sub rosa*, not "in the face" of others that could bear witness. In the case of the *desaparecidos*, operations would usually take place in the middle of the night, with the kidnapping or detention of those marked for disappearance taking place using unmarked cars, with little public fanfare, and the very existence of the procedures immediately denied by the official authorities both in each concrete case and in public discourses by the government authorities.[8] In addition, powerful official injunctions as well as the mere silence surrounding those operations steadily reminded the population about the danger of bearing witness, and dramatically reduced the likelihood that an occasional witness would consider offering public testimony. Further, the very victims of those atrocities, if they survived, made poor witnesses. The destruction of the humanity of the victims through arbitrary detention, rape, torture, and so on, compelled the few surviving victims to silence: their experience lay so beyond the realm of the expected, bypassed so many of the parameters of what is considered "acceptable reality," that those few persons who survived the torture and that, for one reason or another, were subsequently freed, tended to organize their own experiences into two separate realities, two alternative parallel selves.

To function as human beings we require a reasonable amount of coherency or narrative continuity between history, current events and prospection. The drastically discontinuous nature between the experiences of a world of daily atrocities and the daily "normal" social world is such that precludes an integration of the continuum of the personal human experience: former victims of atrocities may just go on living with a discontinuous island of permanent nightmares (what Langer [1991] aptly calls "the ruins of memory").

Returning to the prior argument, the other goal of the repressive regime's silencing procedures is to remind the population about the absolute power of the State and of the risk of any dissent, that is, that it is preferable to accept the State's description about what constitutes reality than to question it or to propose alternative descriptions. In fact, "the first step on the road to total domination is to kill the juridical person in man" (Arendt, 1958, p. 447), that is, "to make the attainment of justice appear hopeless and its pursuit pointless" (Waschler, 1990). Resignation, adaptation, and even indoctrination were preferable or, in some cases, unavoidable. This effect of "thought reform" has been eloquently described in the literature about people who have been under the influence of a cult or sect (Singer & Lalich, 1996), but is in fact one of the most harmful collective effects of living under dictatorships. The ghost of the State becomes ever-present and omniscient.

Both the suppression of the witness (the no-man's land of the disappeared) and the internalized injunction against a critical view were illustrated dramatically during the interview discussed in Chapter 2 and, experientially, during the presentation discussed in this one. The mere public showing of the videotaped interview became, at the same time, blatantly countermanding to those goals, and contributed to exorcising those ghosts.

In fact, an important part of the impact of my presentation can be attributed to the fact that it permitted an act of collective witnessing: the participants were not only witnessing a dramatic, politically, and personally meaningful interview, but also witnessing themselves in the act of being witness.[9] That allowed them to compare themselves before—when the repressive apparatus was in place—and at that moment—where practices of freedom were permitted and even encouraged. Further, they were witnessing themselves in a collective setting that, in the process, mutated from unsafe to safe. The effect of the experience was one of a mending in the fabric of time/space, a realization of a qualitative change in their context, the (re)discovery of the ability to think without internalized bans. That presentation became, in fact, a collective ritual, a ceremony of practices of freedom, a communion of sorts that allowed them to realize, experientially, that in fact freedom was there for them to feel, enact, and enjoy, while carrying with it its unavoidable load of responsibilities. A feature of the interview that resonated intensely with the audience and generated many comments was that the themes touched were extremely hot but their delivery by the family was cool and devoid of any expression of indignation or of blame (to the military junta, to themselves, or to anybody). They were living in their extremely painful circumstances matter of factly, either resigned or surrendered to their hopelessness. To witness that lack of moral indignation, so clearly an effect of the violence of the State, enhanced a reaction of moral indignation on the part of the audience: they themselves had been also victims in one way or another, but they would do something about it.

Still another issue: the family interviewed embodied thousands of families around that country, living in limbo, unable to mourn their dead, unable to go on with their lives. The interview was not only powerful—it dealt openly with politically taboo and emotionally loaded issues—but also clearly therapeutic for the family: it broke down silencing practices, it weaved a series of somatic concerns (an "authorized" code) with words and emotions (an "illegal" code), it canonized until-then ambiguous roles, and so on. And the viewing of the interview was extremely therapeutic for the audience, composed of therapists: it allowed them to witness an instance of therapy as a reparative practice. As the act of witnessing a crime without doing anything about it taints us, shames us, makes us accomplices of the crime, the act of witnessing a therapeutic process and identifying with it contributes to healing us, it repairs us. By extension, it reminded the audience that their own practices had, in many cases, and could have in many others, that same reparative function. Thus, their own healing process after a long period of obfuscation could be channeled through their professional practice: opening their minds to those issues would open their practices to those themes, therapy would become a practice of freedom. The ecology of silence was thus broken. They themselves, extending their help to people who suffered under the violence of state, would be able to mourn while helping others to mourn, to reassume living through helping others do so, to reactivate their thoughts and emotions while defreezing them in others. The same happened, in fact, with members of that family: both grandmother and aunt/mommy became, one year later, actively involved in human rights issues, and in the beginning of what became a protracted criminal trials against the members of the military junta.

"Knowing and not knowing." Those words, uttered during the interview with this family, are also the title of an insightful essay on traumatic memory by Laub and Auerhahn (1993). In massive trauma, these authors point out, the blurring of the boundaries between reality and fantasy evokes emotions of such an intensity that exceeds the capacity of the self to organize reality, or keep itself within bounds. Hence, knowledge, or at least a modicum of certainty about our assumptions about our social world, is voided. Through this effect, "torture destroys the world," that is, the ability to construct a sensible reality (Scarry, 1985). That happened to this family: it didn't require much challenge on my part to show the weakness of the arguments with which they kept denying the extreme likelihood of the death of their loved ones. To acknowledge their death exposed them to an invasion of intense rage, impotence, shame, and fear. It also would allow them to shed the immobility tied to their endless waiting and hoping against hope—akin to those of the families with missing-in-action relatives: they had to confront the need to go on with their lives. They would have, for instance, to redefine the reciprocal roles between adults and children in ways that would enact the permanence of the absence of the disappeared; ultimately, it would seal the relational consequences of their individual lives vis-à-vis one another. For the professional audience, in turn, a parallel process seems to have taken place, and not only by proxy: they too had to shed whatever vestige of denial may have kept them immobilized and frozen, they too had to expose themselves to the flood of their own intense mixed emotions that accompanies the falling of the wall.

The private pain of this family, made into public spectacle by projecting their videotaped interview to a professional audience at a crucial political moment, became a catalytic factor toward a transformative experience. Facilitated by the collective nature of the process, the participants—becoming sometimes actors by identification, sometimes witnesses, sometimes witnesses of others' witnessing—were able to begin to shed a constraint that they had incorporated as a result of years of submersion into a milieu of dictatorship, restricting their capacity to think–feel–act. That process facilitated a responsible reinsertion in their social context that re-legitimized their reparative potential as healers, as agents of change, and as members of a democratic collective.

Notes

1 This effect has also been widely discussed in the debate of whether during WWII the German population was or was not aware of the disappearance and eventual extermination of German Jews. For a powerful and polemical analysis of that issue, see Goldhagen, 1996.

2 It should also be acknowledged, in discharge of the organizers of this congress, that that event had been conceived and announced during a period in which the governing military junta—however debilitated—was still in power, and not everybody was confident that they would yield the site of power to a civilian, democratically elected, president.

3 As mentioned already, this interview had been videotaped with the authorization of the family. The quality of the audio component of the interview was excellent, but the video was rather dark. This proved to be fortunate, as it further preserved the family's anonymity and confidentiality, aided only by the occasional introduction of white noise when the participants provided identificatory verbal information in the course of the conversation. That video has been presented publicly only once, in the context of that convention.

4 I am contrasting it with the powerful experience provided by the late American therapist Norman Paul on two occasions (in the 1970s or early 1980s), once at a congress in Heidelberg, with an audience mainly of young German therapists and, before that, at another professional congress in Philadelphia, in this case mainly with an audience of American family therapists. He briefly told of an artist patient of his who had consulted for a creative block. Upon hearing that he was survivor of the Holocaust, but that his parents—who managed to hide him and arranged his escape as a child—had been killed in the gas chambers of Auschwitz-Birgenau, Paul gave him the task of going to the site of his parents' death and to open his heart by "talking" to them, while carrying with him a cassette recorder to record his testimony. After that brief introduction, Paul placed that cassette in his equipment and let it run without any interruption for its 30-minute duration. In it one could hear the steps of this man resonating on the ceramic floor of the corridors to the gas chambers, while he cries, talks to his parents in English and, I believe, in Polish, and offers for them some prayers in Hebrew—with the occasional background noise of children's voices, probably a school visit to the site. After the tape ended, Paul turned the equipment off and remained in silence.

The 300 or so therapists in the audience did the same—for the following 5 to 10 minutes. One could have heard an insect flying in the silence of that room—only broken by occasional sobbing and nose blowing. Finally the silence was broken by somebody who could not tolerate the tension, and a barrage of sharing of feelings and ideas followed. What an extraordinary emotional and learning experience that was, pregnant with Norman Paul's assumption that those emotionally intense feelings also have a therapeutic value for all—who doesn't have a reason to grieve for somebody or something dear—not to mention it being a powerful example of the value of rituals in therapy!

5 In fact, these immobilizing binds are typical of repressive regimes (and of violence in families), of a mystifying twist by which the State, which is assumed to be the keeper of individual and collective rights, not only violates those very rights but also simultaneously denies that those rights are being violated, silencing dissent and punishing denunciations (Sluzki, 1993). In this regard, see also endnote 7.

6 Emotions, "insofar as they have a moral role, contribute to the preservation of the moral rules of a society" (Armon-Jones, 1986, p. 57). Many emotions, that had been collectively repressed/banned during the prior military dictatorship, were being reawakened through this, and subsequent, collective experience-in-context.

7 It is almost perverse to include only as endnotes many other equally terrible systems of massive human destruction by totalitarian governments, such as the systematic killing of millions of citizens in the Soviet Union under Stalin, the massive Killing Fields during the Khmer Rouge regime in Cambodia, the so-called rehabilitation camps during the Chinese Cultural Revolution, to mention just a few.

8 There are innumerable accounts of very public acts of kidnapping people at work, at school, or in the street taking place in plain daylight. As one of many examples, psychologist Marta Brea, who was by then the director of the Adolescents Department at the Psychiatric Service at the "Araoz Alfaro" Public Hospital at Lanus, Buenos Aires, was picked up on March 30, 1977, by a plain clothes, heavily armed commando with police escort at a staff meeting of that department and taken by force into an unmarked car that left at great speed. Those colleagues who dared to come after them during the procedure were immobilized with submachine guns and the threat: "Get back inside or I'll kill you here and now." She never reappeared.

9 "The listener [. . .] has to be at the same time a witness to the trauma and a witness to himself" (Laub, 1992).

House Taken Over: Culture, Migration and Developmental Cycle in a Moroccan Family Overtaken by Ghosts[1]

4

In the field of family therapy and in other fields in the realm of the behavioral/ social sciences, the professional literature dealing explicitly with cross-cultural issues addresses a dynamic tension between two orientations, namely, *cultural sensitivity* and *cultural specificity* (a debate enriched by crucial contributions by Falicov, 1986, 1998; McGoldrick, 1998; and McGoldrick, Giordano, & Pearce, 2005). The former—cultural sensitivity—emphasizes the need for the therapists to be aware of their own as well as their patients' assumptions about what constitutes reality, about ethical principles, about social relations. In sum, people's perceptions and constructs about the world are strongly influenced by their specific culture, rather than sharing a universal base. Further, many of those assumptions are taken for granted as "the way things are" rather than as beliefs or opinions. Consequently, therapists are encouraged to develop a healthy a priori attitude of "cultural ignorance," refraining from rushing to conclusions, assumptions or certainties in listening to and interacting with the Other in order to reduce the risk of defining as singular or idiosyncratic beliefs or behaviors that may be culture-based, and vice versa. The latter—cultural specificity—recommends that therapists become reasonably informed about the traits of the specific culture of each prospective or actual individual or family that consults in order to increase our contextual understanding, and thus reducing the above-mentioned risks, namely that of falling for what has been known as Type I error—assuming that an outlier, singular element is culture-based when it is idiosyncratic—or Type II error—vice versa (see Falicov, 1986; Avruch, 2003). It also advises that, if the therapist lacks culture-specific knowledge in a given circumstance, it is incumbent upon the therapist to summon the help of cultural brokers familiarized with the patients' culture, including in many cases members of the very family that consults.

This tension entails alternative understandings of what "culture" is about. The richness of this dilemma is fully described by Falicov (2013) when she proposes to categorize the views about the relationship between families and culture in the following four possible sets: (1) *universalist*, representing those who believe that, regardless of their socio-cultural origin and context, "all families (dynamics) are more alike than they are different" (p. 373), leading to a cookie-cutter approach to therapy; (2) *particularist*, that assumes that "families are more different (from one another) than they are alike," leading to a therapeutic stance of educated curiosity and minimalization of assumptions (p. 374); (3) *ethnic-focused*, guided by the belief that "families differ . . . primarily due to one factor: ethnicity" (pp. 374–375) and leading to an important emphasis on exploring those roots as meaningful markers of worldviews; and (4) *multidimensional*, representing the assumption that "families are complex and multidimensional" (pp. 375–376), an ecumenical view that acknowledges the relative impact of a multiplicity of variables—from nature to nurture, from family of origin to circumstantial events, from culture to family idiosyncrasies.

A multidimensional view leads to a complementary rather than mutually exclusive approach vis-à-vis culture: therapists may retain a stance of "cultural ignorance" and minimize value attribution and a priori assumptions, even when presuming a modicum or even a substantial familiarity with a patient's micro and macro culture. Furthermore, therapists are well served by retaining, while interacting with any family, a modicum of "cultural ignorance" even if well informed about that family's specific culture, as each family constitutes a culture-specific world, "culture" including not only ethnic and regional influences in terms of behaviors and social values and assumptions, but also a variety of factors, such as social class and cult-informed distinctions, as well as family traditions and idiosyncrasies.[2] This inclusive approach echoes Gianfranco Cecchin's (1987) recommendation to retain in therapy a permanent stance of "curiosity" as well as Dyche and Zayas' (1995) praise of "naiveté" in clinical practice.

When tracking cultural variables as they impinge upon families, a particularly interesting natural experiment takes place during and following a migration, a process that unavoidably entails a cultural transition, whether expected or dreaded, predicted and welcomed or not by those exposed to it. It could also be said that, in the evolutionary cycle of a family, any family metaphorically migrates from stage to stage even if never moving geographically, as its biologically and culturally determined roles and configurations evolve for each individual and each generation over the life of any given human being. But the progressive timing of all makes it imperceptible in the short run and expected in the long one. In contrast, an actual migration, such as a transition between countries with different embedded rules and expected behaviors, or even from a quaint small town to a metropolis within a given nation, tends to have a much more visible impact. The unavoidable struggle to retain cultural identity and sense of continuity while adapting to a new environment leads to pain, disorientation, and emotional overload, not infrequently translated into intra-familial conflicts, especially across generations, with youngsters tending to represent the values of the new culture and older members the ones of the culture of origin (Sluzki, 1979, 1992a, 1998a; also several contributors in the volume edited by Falicov, 1986).

According to the latest figures (International Office for Migration, 2013), 240 million people worldwide can be labeled as immigrants.[3] More specifically, in the United States, over 40 million people, that is, more than 10% of its total population, is foreign born (Center for Immigration Studies, 2012). Each and all of these individuals have been exposed to the impacts of a cultural transition and the tension between the assumptions, norms, and mores of the culture of origin and those of the culture (in many cases, cultures) of the country of adoption: whatever constitutes "reality" has to be reconstructed and previous assumptions have to be questioned, overimposed on whatever surrounds them, creating ad hoc collages between the familiar and the new. And, while this crisis is normative, those conflicts acquire a specific, distinct face in each family's microcosm.

Hence, the balance needed to avoid falling into Type I or Type II errors (making generic the idiosyncratic or vice versa) requires that the therapist develop the complex ability to become culturally uncertain and actively self-critical while, whenever possible, acquiring some rudimentary knowledge of generic traits of the culture from which families in crisis under their care have emerged. In that quest, our patients can become invaluable cultural brokers.

What follows is a transcription of an interview that I conducted not too long ago in an industrial city in France with a family that had emigrated from Morocco twelve years earlier. The interview took place as a consultation to a team of therapists affiliated with a family therapy center that serves families referred by the judicial system. This clinical material may constitute an appropriate platform to explore some of the cultural crucibles discussed above.

The transcription of the interview is interspersed with comments made immediately after the session to the team that was observing the interview, and subsequently transcribed. Questions that guided these comments—and those analyzing other interventions throughout this book—include the following: (1) How can we navigate the fuzzy boundaries between the tangible and the phantasmagoric or imaginary world of this family without misrepresenting our own beliefs or values, while not contesting the beliefs and values of the family, regardless of how dissonant with ours they may be? In other words, how do we therapists manage, when we do, to avoid the pretense of yielding to a patient's beliefs without imposing our own personal construction of reality? (2) How can we therapists incorporate ourselves into the *themes* of the family? In other words, how can we legitimize ourselves as a participant in the conversational process where the family stories are shared, without imposing our own themes or allowing ourselves to be excessively fascinated by the family's themes, which ultimately hampers our clinical flexibility? (3) How can we therapists destabilize some core narratives associated with a family impasse, facilitating possible changes in family beliefs and interactive styles, without disqualifying elements of their identity? (4) How can we therapists explore professional concerns without risking in the process a violation of the family's view of themselves? (5) What choices must we therapists confront in regard to whether making explicit potentially problematic issues regarding gender roles and behavior without violating cultural boundaries with families raised in cultures where those themes—for instance, the subordinated role of women—are strongly enacted but rarely talked about? (This latter one will become a particularly delicate theme given the dissonance between the cultural values dominant in France, this family's country of adoption, and their own values, clearly rooted in North African/Muslim culture and practices.) (6) How can we therapists be of help without becoming normative when we detect the pains and tribulations of a family that is traversing blindly across significant thresholds in their own individual and collective evolving life cycles, such as, in the family we will discuss, the crisis of an older son entering adolescence while pulled by two distinct cultural expectations? And (7) how can we therapists maintain a balance between our role of professional seeders of ideas and pathways that hold the potential to germinate and our role as witnesses of changes that are already taking place? It merits assuming that the seeds that germinate most richly are those that are already there, in the family's worldview, in which case the role of the therapist is to detect them and help them grow. In fact, in most cases the therapist, rather than being a seeder, is a gardener.

While some of these conceptual issues will be followed up at the end of the chapter, others may remain only as guides for the readers, hoping that they may trigger some musing distilled from their own experience while reading the transcript.

Presentation of the Family and of the Consultation

Rashid, the 16-year-old eldest son of a large family from Morocco that immigrated to France 12 years earlier, appeared one morning with multiple bruises at the local public middle school he attended and where he was considered a good student. A professor, alarmed, reported this situation to the principal of the school, who called the child to his office to find out what happened. Rashid informed him that he had been beaten by his father, and that that was one of many beatings that constituted the habitual disciplinary method used by his father. The director, following prescribed procedures, requested the immediate intervention of the local juvenile protection court authority, and the boy was placed in a public shelter for battered minors. His parents were in turn summoned by social services personnel who interviewed them, evaluated their family situation and informed them that their son would remain in the shelter under their protection. As a condition for an eventual reintegration of the minor to his home, the family was referred to a local mental health center where they would be involved in conjoint family treatment, focusing on the conflicts and current reciprocal animosity between father and child as well as a revision of the policy of violence used in the household for educational purposes.

During the short debriefing that preceded my consultation—again, in the context of a training activity that I was conducting in that town—the middle-aged woman and man therapeutic duo who has been seeing the family already for six sessions described them as a Muslim working-class couple who included a mother, generally marginal, silent and smiling, a father, who kept everybody under his iron-fisted control, and a sea of very well-behaved children surrounding them. The therapists were frustrated by the impervious nature of the father's hegemonic style, who seemed to display expressions of agreement if not of submission to the therapists' recommendations, but managed not to follow any of them. The therapists described also their futile efforts at improving family communication by attempting to make the family members speak to one another, without much success. Disheartened by their sense of lack of change, the therapists volunteered the family for a consultation with me, taking advantage of the fact that I was visiting their city to lead a workshop on family interventions. When I asked the therapists what were their expectations about this consultation, they expressed their wish to be guided on how to speak with this family without becoming infuriated with the father and, broadly speaking, to find a silver lining in the cloud of their own sense of hopelessness. As the debriefing was ended they added, almost as an aside, that several of the siblings in this family were hallucinating, a situation that they had avoided dealing with; however, they were interested in my view as a psychiatrist as they pondered the need for a referral to explore the use of neuroleptic medication.

After expressing my appreciation to the two therapists for bringing the family to my attention and for the information provided, I repeated to them my understanding of what were *their* own expectations and invited them to tell me afterwards whether the consultation ended up being useful for them in that regard. I then asked them how they had framed this consultation with me to the family. They answered that they told them that an international expert was visiting their agency to provide consultations and they wanted to benefit from his opinion about the progress of the therapy.

I invited the two therapists to join me and the family for the consultation and to participate freely during the interview. They answered that they would be happy to sit in but preferred to see me work rather than to intervene. I agreed.

The Interview

In the hallway the therapists introduced me as well as a volunteer interpreter (that I had requested just in case my mediocre French failed me) to the family. I greeted them individually and invited them into the consultation room. They entered in the following order: father, youngest daughter, daughter who follows in age, mother, two other daughters in order of increasing age, third son in order of age, eldest son, and finally second son, followed by the two family therapists, the interpreter and myself. They sat in a semi-circle, with the parents in the center, the daughters on one side, and the sons on the other. The local co-therapist team sat marginally, indicating in that way their subordinated position of observers. I sat facing that semi-circle, and my interpreter sat by me. The mother was covered from head to toe with European clothing—trousers, raincoat, shawl, leaving only her face and hands uncovered.[4] All the rest were dressed in a European informal and rather conservative style and all the girls used a headscarf. The children were well disciplined and attentive.

I conducted the interview in French (with the occasional help of the interpreter, who translated for me into English whenever I signaled to her that I had failed to understand a word or complete a sentence). The conversational style of the consultation was characterized by many overlapping utterances throughout the interview, both in the exchanges in French with me and in simultaneous conversations in French and Arabic within the family. The father spoke quite fluent French, with a strong North African accent, and he expressed himself with intensity and vehemence. The mother, contained and modest, smiled timidly when I addressed her, tended to answer with monosyllables, and often signaled that she did not understand me, and promptly her husband would translate for her from French into Arabic, she would answer in Arabic and he would translate for her into French to me.

The following text contains the complete transcription of the session, interspersed with commentaries about the therapeutic process.

Therapist:	(While I sat down) This colleague (the translator), who is also a family therapist, is here to help me with the language, because, unfortunately, my French is not too good. Well, thank you very much for having accepted my having this conversation with you.
Father:	No, no, thanks to *you*.
T.:	(To F., signalling the rest of the family) What a large crowd you bring with you!
F.:	(With a proud tone) And only half of them came! The other half stayed at home.
T.:	You two have a true battalion of children!
F.:	This is how our life is. Because our parents have also done it, they had many children.
T.:	Is your family of origin, the one where you were raised, very large?
F.:	We were 14, ten alive and four dead. We were 14.
T.:	And in this current family?
F.:	They all are alive.
T.:	I am glad to hear that. And in your family, ma'am?
	(F. speaks in Arabic with his wife, apparently translating my question.)
Mother:	My mother has 12, seven alive and five dead (she had some added exchanges in Arabic with her husband, apparently continuing with the theme).
T.:	(to both) Have you thought of having more children?
F.:	No, with the 13 we have is enough.
T.:	13 is a good number; it is a magical number.

I introduced the word "magical" inspired by the information provided by the therapists that in this family there were several children who have hallucinations, in preparation for possible reformulations. And perhaps I was already conjured by that interesting way of counting dead and alive as co-equal members of the family.

F.:	Good magic, I hope, because some type of magic may be problematic, magic may bring problems.
T.:	And your . . . (I begin to address a question toward the child sitting to my left, but F. anticipates my move and interrupts me)
F.:	This (starting from the edge of the semicircle) is Karim. This (he doesn't mention his name) is the oldest one (he seem to shift to a chronological sequence), then Hassan, then Karim, then comes **** (names in Arabic that I do not understand), then Apria, then ****, then ****, then Emal, then Sounia, then Salema, and then ****. And the little one, two months old, stayed at home.
T.:	And by what logic did you decide which child should come and which should stay at home?

Throughout the interview I address some of my questions to the father, some to the parental couple, some to another particular member, and some to the whole group. However, the father answered the majority of the questions. I do not interfere with this style, which I assume culture-driven, though occasionally I will simply repeat my question until the addressee answers.

F.:   I only brought the people who have the problem, the problem of the phenomenon. Rashid (now he mentions his name) has the phenomenon, Hassan has the phenomenon, Karim has the phenomenon, Apria has the phenomenon, Emal has the phenomenon, Sounia has the phenomenon and Salema has the phenomenon. But Rashid (pointing at him expressively and with a bitter voice) is the one with the big problem.

I.:   So the oldest son has the biggest problem. It sounds reasonable. And what is the problem or, rather, for whom is this problem a problem?

F.:   The problem began . . . (to the wife) when did we buy the house? (Short conversation in Arabic) . . . began two years ago. After we bought the house there were no problems for four years, and suddenly the problem started. A dog appeared in the house. Rashid has seen the dog, Apria has seen the dog, Emal has seen the dog, Sounia has seen the dog, and Salema has seen the dog.

Rashid: (to T.) I also had an experience in which I saw a woman with a knife wanting to attack me as well as the younger ones (an animated conversation in Arabic ensues, while I double-check with the translator whether they are referring to a factual dog or to a vision of a dog. She isn't sure either.).

T.:   Was it like a ghost?

R.:   I woke up scared; there was a woman with hair made of worms or snakes that wanted to kill me with a knife.

T.:   Like a Medusa? Ah, it was something like a nightmare! Was that woman or ghost in the same plot or dream or fantasy as the dog?

"Ghost," "nightmare," "fantasy," as well as the previous word "magical," are introduced as alternative benign labels for what the therapists of this family seemed to have defined as possible severe psychiatric symptoms.

R.:   Yes, but it continued to appear later. When I want to sleep it reappears and does not want to disappear. Every time I want to sleep . . .

T.:   Aha, whenever you want to start sleeping it reappears! How unpleasant!

R.:   Yes, very unpleasant.

T.:   And what is the relationship between that nightmare and the one of the dog?

R.:   It happened in the same room in which I saw the black dog. And she (Apria) has also seen the black dog.

I notice that the label "nightmare"—a shift aimed mainly at reducing the concerns of the silent-but-present couple of therapists, who had expressed clinical preoccupation about this manifestation—seems to be becoming accepted into the conversation.

T.:   (To Apria) You also? Were you awake or asleep?

Apria: I was awake, in the same room, at night.

T.:   Ah, it is a collective nightmare . . . but some of you seem to have been awake during that time.

F.:   I am going to explain it to you. He (Rashid, again unmentioned by name) saw the woman. Apria saw a man and a dog. Sounia saw a man and a dog. Emal saw the dog and she covered her head, out of fear, with her bed sheets, and on the following day . . . she was normal the previous day, and when she woke up she was cross-eyed.

T.:   Oh, yes?

F.:   Yes, but now, after her surgery, she is fine again.

T.:   Oh! Did she have surgery? (I called Emal with a gesture; she approached me confidently; I held her head in a friendly gesture, looked at her eyes, performed a quick exploration of convergence eye movements—that is, I asked her to look at my finger and slowly moved it to the bridge of her nose and back—I thanked her, and sent her back to her seat.)

The topic of the nightmares and the information that the children were, not surprisingly due to their number, sharing rooms worried me; more specifically, it made me think about the possibility of incest. My interaction with the young girl (and later with another one of the daughters), who tolerated without any discomfort my being close to her and my touching her face, reduced my worries, as I didn't perceive any tattle-tale behaviors such as mistrust, rejection, fear, or seductive behavior in the children or alarm in any of the adults: they all behaved appropriately to the situation.

F.:   One year later Sounia also saw the dog and she also became cross-eyed. She also had to have surgery. The same thing happened to this one (pointing at Apria) after the phenomenon occurred to her.

T.:   (To Apria) Really? Did you also see the dog and later had problems with your eyes? (To Rashid) What about you? Didn't you have problems with your eyes after the dog visited you?

R.:   No, I did not have problems, but my vision has diminished.

T.:   (To Apria) And this happened also to you after the dog visited you? (With a gesture, I invited her to approach me, she did so, and I took off her glasses and examined her sight; she collaborated without mistrust.) Aha, it is the left eye (I gestured appreciation and she returned to her place).

F.:   All four of them have the problem in their left eye. Last year, it happened to the youngest. I had risen for dawn prayers, and I found her with her head covered by a blanket. I asked her "What happened to you?" and she answered "I am scared, because I saw the dog under the wardrobe." Since then she always covers herself. I talked to a Muslim counselor about the problem of the phenomenon, and he recommended that I should read the Koran. I did it, every morning I read a bit of the Koran, and things are improving. There are walls in the house that make noise, cupboards that crack, but overall things are getting better. All of this has been happening during the last two years.

T.:   How do you explain all of that?

F.:   You see, before us, there was a disabled person living in that house, and he had a dog.

T.:   What about yourself? Do you have a dog in the house?

F.:   No, we don't have a dog. We Muslims cannot have dogs inside the house; only out in the garden, because we say that when a dog enters the house, the angels cannot come in. Cats can be in the house, but dogs cannot.

T.:   Aha, so you have to choose between dogs and angels. And who has *not* seen the dog?

F.:   He (Hassan) has not seen it, he (Karim) has not seen it, and also ***, ****, and ***** haven't seen it either.

T.:   So the family could be divided between those who have seen the dog and those who did not see it. Have you yourself seen the dog?

To organize a whole group of those "who have seen the dog" allows placing Rashid as part of a set, instead of isolating him, and de-pathologizes the experience, a move furthered by this last question, addressed to the father.

F.:   I am going to tell you. While still in Morocco I have seen a wolf in the house, and all the little ones—my younger brothers and sisters—ran to me so that I could protect them. I have seen it twice.

T.:   But fortunately it didn't have any physical effect on you, correct? (He shook his head in denial) What about you, ma'am? Have you had these types of experiences?

F.:   She hasn't had those experiences (she nodded in agreement).

T.:   So the family contains two complementary sectors, a balance that may be extremely useful in life.

Vague as this statement may be, to define both family sectors as complementary expands the attempt at increasing the complexity of the narrative, expanding it into a richer system of checks and balances.

F.:   Yes, the sector around me and the sector that is with her, and some kids in-between.

T.:   Now, for you, Hassan, considering that you haven't had that kind of visual experience, this *not* having had it, is it something that you consider positive, that is, good, or is it something negative, something that you would like to have?

This question conveys the notion that I do not take for granted that "the phenomenon" is bad (moreover, I call it a "visual experience," a benign label). It also takes away the assumption of "badness" attached to that experience and transforms it into an opinion.

Hassan:	It is good.
T.:	Aha, it is good. (To Karim) And for you?
Karim:	It is also good.
T.:	And for you, ma'am?
F.:	It is good (she smiled and nodded).

As mentioned above, I interfered only minimally with this pervasive pattern of the husband speaking for the wife and for some of their children as I probably would have done, one way or another, with a Western-cultured family that I would see in my clinical practice. The reason for this restraint is that I saw it less as an idiosyncratic act of control on the part of the man than as the enactment of a patriarchal cultural practice. However, I would challenge it here and there by repeating a question addressed to somebody else when answered by the father, as will be seen below.

T.:	Ah, I asked that question because I was thinking that you, Hasan, would perhaps feel excluded from this experience, like: "What happens with me, that I cannot have these magical experiences?"
F.:	Yes, yes, but for me it is not magic, it is a misfortune. Allow me to explain: there is magnificent magic and there are bad things. After the phenomenon occurred, I had problems with the oldest one: lack of communication. Before that he was magnificent, but after the phenomenon he is like a foreigner in our house.
T.:	(To Rashid) Are you also experiencing this distancing? (F. seems to explain to R. in Arabic what I have said—and sometimes I appreciated that role as, let's admit it, my French is far from perfect!)
F.:	Yes, the same experience.
T.:	(To Rashid, for the second time) Do you also have the same experience, of distancing, with your father?
R.:	Yes, yes.

This is one of my many attempts, in the course of the session, to keep talking to the specific members of the group until they answer directly to me, gently attempting to challenge the (collective) pattern that retains the father's hegemony.

T.:   (To R.) For how long have you experienced that distance? (F. translates the question into Arabic.)

R.:   For five years approximately.

T.:   Did it begin before or after the experience?

R.:   Before, I mean, after I had the vision of this woman with the knife who was not walking but flying.

T.:   Aha, how have you explained that effect?

R.:   Since then I cannot stay in the house, it's as if she was there.

T.:   What have you tried to do against this vision, and the anguish that comes with it?

The tie vision emotion continues my effort at reducing the risk of labeling the son's experience as "a symptom." This emphasis was aimed more at the present-but-silent therapist than at the family, for whom those visions did not carry a toxic label.

R.:   My father said that I should read the Koran. And I went to the Mosque, and prayed. But the effect stayed. This woman does not appear any more, but I have other nightmares in which the devil appears and comes to attack my little brothers and I have to defend them.

T.:   This type of dream is, from your own point of view, positive or negative?

This type of circular question continues my efforts to destabilize the dominant narrative. Furthermore, I chose the nightmare for its focus, a potentially negative experience that could also be interpreted positively (as a "heroic" theme, as I will say later).

R.:   Negative.

T.:   (To F.) And from your point of view?

F.:   Negative.

T.:   (To Hassan) And from your point of view? Is it also negative?

Hassan: Yes, yes.

Exploring the point of view of the different members of the family has a dually important function: it not only allows each one to have a voice, but also "positive" and "negative" are transformed into opinions instead of being intrinsic attributes of these dreams.

T.:   I ask you because there are many people, not religious but scientific, who say that having the possibility of having dreams and even nightmares is very positive, it is like having a good connection with our complex interior world. Moreover, there are people who *interpret* dreams so they can read the inner conflicts, that type of thing.

"Dreaming is good" is an affirmation that attaches a positive sign to a good part of the experiences that we were discussing. It was, though, phrased mildly, as it entailed a challenge to the father's views (and perhaps—I simply didn't know—to their cultural/religious assumptions).

F.:   Yes, yes, yes. I understand it very well, but for us it is the opposite thing. Among us, in Morocco, there are good phenomena and bad phenomena. But the boys have not had good phenomena. For example this one (Rashid), until he had the phenomenon he was fine—he was good, kind, communicative, serious—he had the character of a 40-year-old person, he was taking care of his brothers and sisters without problems, very well, magnificent, he was in first place. But, after the phenomenon, he was bad; he confronts everybody, he is nervous, contradicts everyone, gets angry, fights, and creates a real wall between him and me.

T.:   However, if I understood it correctly, the last nightmare that he described was a noble dream, as he was protecting his little siblings, he was kind to them and responsible. Did I understand it correctly?

F.:   Yes, yes, yes, but he continues with the barrier.

I continue fearlessly with my positive description.

T.:   I believe that this family is blessed with a special capacity, that of expressing many emotions through the world of dreams. In fact, an activity that you might turn out to find useful and what is done in many cultures would be to gather together everybody every morning—magic dreamers and concrete dreamers alike—to tell each other your dreams.

I have shifted from confrontation of views to proposing a ritual—not expecting them to follow it as much as to draw a scenario in their own imagination where such exchange would be possible while creating another more encompassing umbrella, that of the dreamers (whether magic or not), in another attempt at decontaminating of the experience of the nightmares as well as placing Rashid and father under the same label.

F.:   Yes. What I do when they have the nightmares is to read the Koran. But
            he continues having the nightmares.
            (Rashid begins to talk but I interrupt him)
T.:   (To Hassan) Do you remember your dreams?
Hassan: Yes.
T.:   (To Karim) and you?
Karim: Yes.
T.:   Ah, what a magnificent possibility you all have, that of remembering your
            dreams!
Rashid: (Interrupting) Since we moved into this house we share a bedroom with
            my brothers, and I always have the same dream, the one I told you, in
            a very long corridor, always the same one. I wake up and continue see-
            ing the appearance of the devil, it looks at me, but it wants to attack my
            brothers, I defend them, and . . . it is always the same dream.
T.:   Did you tell someone about this dream?
Rashid: No, I really didn't tell it to anybody.
T.:   Well, I believe that, to complement the readings of the Koran, the idea of
            talking about the dreams may deserve consideration, because the world
            of the dreams is a rich world. There are people who never remember
            their dreams. I have several children, not as many as you but several.
            Two of them never remember their dreams; even when they have a night-
            mare they wake up and forget the content! And the fact that they don't
            remember their dreams makes me very sad. It is like a loss of . . . collec-
            tive capital. Aside, in the world of dreams there is no authority: nobody
            can say: "You must dream this way, or that way."
F.:   (Quite enthusiastic) Among us, Ber Bahab says: "Dreams are to be stud-
            ied." One learns much from dreams.
T.:   (To F.) The dreams cause harm only when one conceals them, isn't it
            so? When they are shared, it is good for everyone. The toughest dreams
            are softened when one tells them. (To Mother) Ma'am, you, if I under-
            stood correctly, are one of those that do not have intense dreams. But
            the division must not be so sharp. I imagine that you, intense or not,
            also have dreams, isn't that true? (Silence. Mother and father look at
            each other.)
F.:   She did not understand what you said. (She smiled) No, she does not
            have intense dreams, it is another style, she just dreams of things, of
            what happened the day before (Rashid helped in this description adding
            a couple of words in French that his father was seeking, and with short
            translations into Arabic to his mother of what his father was saying, who
            smiled).
T.:   (To the mother) Aha, you have less symbolic dreams.
F.:   Yes, yes. I, on the other hand, when someone dies, I dream it, I bury them
            in my dreams.
T.:   Aha, so there is clearly a sector of the family that is more magical in its
            dreams, and another one that is more concrete and realistic.
F.:   I, for example, when someone is going to die, I dream it in advance, and
            in the morning, when I wake up, I tell my wife, "You know what? There
            is someone who is packing his bag to go on a long trip," like that, in jest.

T.:   (To father) After you, who is the person with the longest history of powerful dreams, including dreams that have negative aspects? After you, who is the second person in the family that has this type of virtue, this quality?

This question—one of order or sequence, also in the tradition of circular questions—was formulated at preparing the reintroduction of the theme of Rashid as second to his father. However, once again, a surprise awaits me.

F.:   I believe it is my brother.
T.:   Aha. And in *this* family?
F.:   I don't think anybody.

I do not have any other option but to introduce the idea myself.

T.:   What about him? (Rashid).
F.:   But he has bad dreams, nightmares.
T.:   They were not only bad dreams.
R.:   I also have good dreams.
T.:   This is what I am talking about. Do you tell your family about your good dreams or only about the nightmares?
R.:   No, only the nightmares.
T.:   (To F.) That is why I have the impression that maybe Rashid is the second person after you that has this power, this virtue.
F: I also thought this about him before: he is the oldest one, he is the chief, and he is going to have the responsibility of the family, the one who directs the family, deals with the boys when we go out. He is the one that is the chief . . . but then he ended everything.

While re-running a previous theme, a new emotional climate and thematic tension is developing in the conversation: the father's tone of voice has more sadness than anger. However, my impression is that he is too offended by Rashid's distancing and refusal to obey him to accept my suggestion of including Rashid in the group he belongs to—that of the magic dreamers. Following that impression, I attempt to open up again the issue explicitly.

T.:   (To Rashid) It seems to me that, for reasons that are not very clear to me, you, Rashid, talk only about your nightmares, about the negative dreams, and not about others. But, as you yourself said, you also have other dreams, good dreams, a rich interior life (Rashid: Yes, yes), like your father has. So, maybe "the problem of communication" is that your father mentioned includes your having chosen for a while now not to open all the other dreams to the rest of the family, an opening that might show to your father that you are the second great dreamer. I have the impression that you have chosen for a while not to be his successor.

With this comment I condense the theme of dreams and the issues of family hierarchy and of obedience to the cultural mandates that are required to fulfill the expectations of delegated responsibility in the family order, an issue mentioned by the father as the source of his resentment.

F.:   It is like that, exactly, it is like that.
T.:   (To R.) At what age did you choose, temporarily, not to be your father's successor?

To have defined the position of Rashid as volitional (". . . you have chosen . . .") seems to have made acceptable the formulation. Notice also the incorporation of the word "temporarily" (and, in the prior formulation, "for a while") that introduces the hope of the potential reversibility or at least change of the situation.

R.:   At the age of 12. (A conversation in Arabic between father and son follows, apparently centered in dates.)
F.:   At the age of 12.
T.:   Maybe at the age of 12 it is a very heavy load (F. helps my formulation by providing me in French the word "heavy"!) to be the successor, the chief of the family. At that age, one wants to play, to be with friends.
F.:   It is just.
T.:   Not only is it just but maybe also reasonable. "I want to play with my friends, and not be in charge of the house." This decision by you, Rashid, however reasonable, seems to have had complicated effects, as it must have left a hole in the family. (A silence ensues) Is there someone who has occupied that place of number two?
F.:   It is Hassan.
T.:   (To H.) You are Hassan, yes?
Hassan: Yes.
T.:   Now, pardon me for not knowing how these things are done, but, if your brother would decide to recapture this position . . . if Rashid would tell you, Hassan, "OK, I decided to finish my strike of five years" . . . (Now to Rashid) If you would choose to finish your strike, do you think it could be difficult for your brot her to give up his current position of power, or maybe, I don't know, perhaps *to share* it?

"Sharing" is a very tentative idea that I floated around, since I don't even know whether it is culturally applicable.

R: Yes, I think so, but I don't want to do it (i.e., to re-claim the duties of the first-born male) now.

T.:   Yes, yes, indeed, I respect your position, this was only a hypothetical question. And you (to Hassan), what do you think? If your brother would decide to re-claim his position as your father's second-in-command, would it be difficult for you?

H.:   For me it is the same, if my father wants it.

F.:   But *I* would not accept it. I would not agree to share it.

T.:   (To F., with a tender and understanding tone of voice) More than angry, you are offended with Rashid.

F.:   Not offended, but it is he (Rashid) who has to make the effort to share it.

T.:   What you say is very wise, because you seem to understand some of Rashid's dilemma. Aside, unless he wants it and makes the effort, it would be an uneven share of the burden.

Though the focus of the father is in "it is he," I underline "to share," in order to be able to continue with the topic of the overload of the role of first-born, that looks to me as a theme with transformative potential: to be "the person in charge of the whole family" Moroccan style may have become an excessive if not dissonant expectation for a teenager raised in France. Of course, I also smuggled the possibility that father understands Rashid's dilemma—did he ever have it himself? Does he secretly admire him for rebelling?

F.:   Yes, I know it well. But what I do not know is why he stopped communicating with me. If he wants now to return to be the chief of the family, I would not accept it, but I would be willing for them to share it.

Father seems to have made a shift, and is offering an interesting, novel olive branch.

T.:   Very wise, certainly. It may be a way of avoiding the excessive weight of the whole responsibility on one person's shoulder, in addition to allowing you to welcome once more into your bosom a son that you miss.

The introduction of the emotional tone is not questioned by the father.

F.:   Because now it is he (Hassan) who has the power and the responsibility of the house.

T.:   (To Rashid) So it is up to a point *your* choice to decide whether to open this other, more tender, part of you—your good dreams—and reconnect with the family without having to overburden yourself. But let it be clear, as with many other changes in life, if you decide to finish your strike, it would be very important that you do it very slowly, perhaps just by beginning to describe also, as you did here, your noble dreams, and your hopes and projects. Because I believe your father values very much this virtue of having access to the most creative aspects of the dreams. Maybe you, ma'am, might help your son in this process (exchange in Arabic between father and mother).

It seems abundantly clear to me that the metaphor of the "good dreams," a positive attitude from and toward Rashid, and his re-incorporation to a certain "natural order" of the family as well as the potential emotional welcome of the father have all become intertwined subjects.

F.:   Yes, but he has cut the communication also with her, not only with me. He is like a foreigner with everybody.

I ponder: is Rashid a representative of the culture of the adopted country? Are they involved in a Lévi-Straussian structural equation in which Rashid is for the rest of the family as the family is for France?

T.:   I understand it. It is hard to be a foreigner. I know it myself very well. (A comfortable short silence ensues.) But, a moment ago, I asked your son whether he would be interested in opening this part of the world of his dreams, and he said that he was. If this is the case (to Rashid), I am inviting your mother to be the one who can help you to open up. (F. seems to be translating word by word to his wife what I say.) But you have established a precedent of five years of strike, and it may not be easy to shift, and even for others in your family to accept, a different behavior and a different role, different for them as well as for you.

F.:   (While looking at R. with a friendly gaze, who in turn is looking at him openly) We can try.

I had been pondering when to end the interview, and decided to do it at that moment, so as to anchor the affirmation of the father, that was uttered with a thoughtful and conciliatory tone.

T.:   (To the whole family) Well, we will have to stop here. This has been a very rich conversation. (I then address to the family's stable co-therapists, until then silent.) I appreciate very much your being here, and I would also appreciate very much if you could send me a letter in two or three months so I could know if this exchange of ideas has been useful for this family and even for you. This family has a special virtue, the capacity to connect with the magical inner world. This is important and valuable, even if it risks connecting with negative experiences.

F.:   Among us, the Muslims, the Koran says that it is necessary to accept the good things and the bad things; the phenomena exist.

T.:	I hope that my suggestions have been harmonic with the Koran.
F.:	All the sacred books are wise and have similar ideas, the Bible, the Talmud, and the Koran. In Morocco, there are Jewish doctors who give medicines to the Muslims and read the Torah to them.
T.:	(Smiling) And there are family therapists who sometimes fulfill also these functions.

The French team of co-therapists make a closing speech, expressing their appreciation to the family and to me for our participation. We all stood up and greeted each other formally and affectionately.

F.:	(While shaking hands with the therapists and with me) In dreams, problems appear and within dreams, solutions also appear.
T.:	Wise once again.
	(The family leaves).

Discussion: Culture, Migration, Social Network and Life Cycle

This material could be utilized as a platform of exchanging ideas about universal issues in our daily clinical practice, such as tensions intrinsic to a family life cycle, issues of gender (expressed in different ways in different subcultures), the potential clash between the bio-psycho-social and the medical models, and, in general terms, the vicissitudes of the healing process. It could also be discussed in terms of problems of adaptation in families that have transferred from one cultural context to another, and issues that arise when families who consult us come from cultures with which we may not be very familiar. Indeed, acculturation is a central background topic of this interview. In fact, this family has not only migrated but also done so into a culture that is discontinuous to theirs both in terms of language and of habits. This is reflected in a transparent way during the interview: a family with extreme internal cohesion, upheld within a very authoritarian centralized paternal hegemony, and with clear borders with implicit and explicit distinctions between "in" and "out," "we" and "others." The dearth of outside (exo-cultural) connections made the isolation of the wife–mother in this family particularly dramatic: she was triply alienated by the trans-cultural distance between her immediate family and milieu and her extended social environment, by the contrasting role of women between both cultures, and by her lack of knowledge of the dominant language in their country of adoption—probably a cause and result of the other two variables. As could be predicted—and it was confirmed in conversation with their designated therapists—this family lived in a neighborhood that was predominantly Moroccan, and retained a social network that was consonant with theirs.

Specifically, the mother's social exchanges—with neighbors as well as in her exchanges in local shops and markets—would take place with people who shared her language and habits, while the infrequent incursions into the larger city would take place escorted by her husband or several of their children, with minimal other social exchanges. In terms of the father, aside from contacts at work, where he was exposed to and interacting with people of a variety of extractions, his social life was mainly confined to his family, and those who frequented his mosque. In fact, had I not been informed otherwise in advance, a good part of their social behaviors and external appearances would have made me believe that they had immigrated only a few months ago, rather than twelve years ago. In all appearances, they have relentlessly kept out of their dwelling the "dogs" of the surrounding European culture with reasonable success until their older child incorporated expectations of that culture during high school.

As mentioned above, in most immigrant families who experience cross-cultural and language barriers, children and adolescents are the vehicle of entry into the new culture. It could be reasonable to hypothesize that, in this family, the older offspring—the first who has been socialized in the schools of the country of adoption—must have been the prime importer of the new norms and mores into the family, and that role may have strongly determined the collective process leading to his disaffiliation to the family's cultural tradition and the multilayered family crisis it triggered.

The decision of the Social Services to define this problem as one of intra-familial violence and to recommend family therapy as a condition for reintegration of the minor to his family can be criticized as well as praised. It may be criticized from a Foucaultian perspective, because of their use of psychiatry as a means for social control. The therapists' concerns about "hallucinations," which clearly were collective, culture-facilitated nightmares along the style of *pavor nocturnus,* may be an inkling of the same, or an example of the temptation of therapists to express their own clinical frustrations by escalating diagnostic labels. That decision can also be criticized by the absence of a more pragmatic cross-cultural perspective that would have favored a more informative/educational approach, such as summoning the father and informing him that in France it is against the law to beat a child no matter what the family's culture of origin accepts, and warning him about the legal consequences of repeating that behavior—leaving aside the question of whether this approach is an effective educational inforcement method. In fact, only one country, as far as this author knows, Israel, educate immigrants (with mixed results, though) about the legal norms and mores of the country they are adopting plus an immersion experience in the native language—while there are a number of other countries that offer a perfunctory introduction to some of these norms only during the acquisition of citizenship. The intervention of the local Social Services agency triggered by the school report of a child being severely beaten by his father, and the subsequent removal of the son from the family household by the judicial authority, may be defined as harsh acculturation by default conveying the message: "In France, physical violence with children is not allowed." And the father behaved submissively to the authorities of his country of adoption (represented, among others, by the therapists themselves, as the therapy was mandated and not sought), but was stonewalling, to the dismay of the therapists, any suggestion that may challenge what for him was a reasonable behavior, rooted in his own culture and childhood experiences, and replicated in his own authoritarian style with his family.[5]

The course of this interview portrays, microcosmically, a two-way process of acculturation. First, my position of active ignorance and adaptive respect to their culture-informed behavior educated me about some cultural assumptions and the style of the family, to which I yielded, broadly speaking. This stance allowed me to progressively become a legitimate interlocutor of the stories offered by the family and a credible, reliable source of counterpoints.[6] In turn, this allowed me to introduce, progressively, in a gentle, non-abrasive way, comments and interactive behaviors that challenged some of their cultural assumptions that seemed to be accepted, or at least not openly rejected by the father, as spokesperson for the old culture, and by the family as a whole. Among them may be listed: the recognition of the difficulties entailed in the role of "number one son," the idea of sharing the leadership, soliciting opinions instead of giving orders, the legitimacy of each other's voice, reciprocal respect regardless of age—all norms that I enacted (not forced or preached) during the interview. My behavior, hopefully, conveyed to the family, or at least to the therapists who were witnessing the session, the notion that a good process of acculturation entails being able to internalize new norms without disconnecting or denigrating the original ones.[7] That was facilitated also by the language of ghosts chosen by Rashid to enact or express his rebellion, which resonates with his parents' culture and experience—the story of the father protecting his siblings from a ghostly wolf must have been an account known to all of them.

Follow-up Information

Following my request, ten months after this interview I received a letter from the therapists in which they informed me about the evolution of this family. "Your participation," they wrote, "has been a very enriching experience, since it allowed all of us—family and therapists alike—to put in perspective our infallibility, until then not questioned. The fact that we needed to consult someone made us more human in their eyes, and allowed us to accompany them in their process of change, rather than attempt to guide it . . . that elicited only reluctance on their part. The nightmares continue appearing every now and then, and we have the impression not only that they are a family language but also that they are used instrumentally to retain the contact with us. The dynamics of the family has changed considerably: the father seems more willing to listen to his children, reducing his moralizing sermons, and has even recognized in front of his wife and children past mistakes. The daughters also participate more actively and they make themselves heard. We were not very surprised when there was a relapse: two months after the session with you, the father gave another beating to Rashid, but since then there hasn't been any more violence. The father continues using some medicinal Moroccan plants and occasionally he relies on his religious/healer counsel. Rashid has returned to live with the family, and maintains a good attitude and contact with his father. Both sons and daughters display excellent school performance and they are proud of their grades. Finally, the family asked us a couple of times what was your opinion about them . . . and we have soothed them with praises."

Notes

1 The title of this chapter, while pertinent per se to this family's story, has an added cultural resonance for the author: "Casa tomada" ("House taken over") is the title of a rather surreal, fascinating, well-known short story by the Argentine writer Julio Cortazar (1985), with a minimalist plot: an elderly brother and sister, living together, progressively restrict their living area almost without talking about it, closing one door of their house after another as rooms in their house are intuited by them to become occupied by the (never seen or specified) "others." The reader may find this outstanding story in English at jessbarga.wikispaces. com/file/view/Cortázar,+House+Taken+Over.pdf.

2 For a fascinating story of discovery of the roots of a family's rituals, cf. Alexy, 1993.

3 Most countries have their own legal definition of what constitutes a "foreigner" and an "immigrant." To provide some cross-national frame, the UN Population Division defines a migrant as someone living outside her country of birth or citizenship for 12 months or more (*Migration News*, 2003).

4 Mother and the children thus convey the double inscription of Muslim and of Europeanization, perhaps as a signal of their cultural transition, perhaps as a choice to muffle the religious/ethnic signal sent by the use of traditional garments in order to blend in a society where they are a disadvantaged and discriminated minority.

5 Nuha Abudabbeh (2005) describes a Muslim/Arab "family type" as patriarchal and authoritarian, with pyramidal hierarchy according to age and gender, scarce horizontal communication, with prevalence of rationale based on obligations and self-sacrifice at the service of the family group and of the widespread family. Parents communicate with offspring through lessons, challenges, and punishments rather than dialogue, and children are expected to self-censor expressions of distress or rebellion about parental rules and styles of discipline. The mother is generally the messenger between father and children. Chastity is a dominant value, and incest is very infrequent. This overall description fits the case.

6 The etymological Latin root of "interlocutor" is *inter,* "between," and *locutor,* "speaker(s)." It is in this virtual in-between, interpersonal locus where a basic consensus can be reached about key premises of a shared reality, a solid platform that allows the development of alternative, better fitting stories about that very reality (Sluzki, 1997; Cobb, 2013).

7 During the discussion that followed this interview with the participants in the workshop, who had witnessed it via closed circuit, a colleague accused me of complicity with the patriarchal structure of the family for not having challenged the man's hegemony and not having provided enough voice to his wife by blocking his usurpation of her turns. To that I answered that I didn't yield to the temptation to do so beyond what I did (attempting on several occasions to address her directly, and defining a crucial role for her in the process of reconnection of the alienated son) as that would have almost assured my alienation from the man if not from the whole family and the possibility of doing something—not everything— for and with them.

The Ancient Cult of Madame: When Therapists Trade Curiosity for Certainty

5

In the early 1960s, a year after I graduated from medical school, still very wet behind my ears, I was awarded a small grant to conduct an experimental trial of what by then was a new neuroleptic medication (Sluzki, 1961). At the dawn of the second generation of phenothiazines, this study involved a cohort of chronic psychiatric patients at the main psychiatric hospital for men in Buenos Aires, a rather dismal warehousing facility with thousands of inmates, until then treated with little more than confinement, neglect, and occasional electroshocks. One of these patients, with whom I established a cordial and fond relationship, was a lucid man with a running diagnosis of paraphrenia[1] who had been involuntarily committed by judicial mandate several years before—he had harassed a Supreme Court Justice while trying to make him listen to his scheme in a rather passionate way, an episode that sealed his destiny. A former trumpet player, he was involved from dusk to dawn in an extremely rich and complex organization that he had created with the aim of bringing talented people together to save the world from meanness, cruelty, and abuse. His sweetly naïve methodology, a variation of a Ponzi scheme, consisted of convincing ten persons that mean people were mean and should be ignored; each of the ten recruits would convince another ten individuals, and so on. As a consequence, in the long run, dictators, exploiters, and other mean people would become socially and economically ostracized and, presto, peace in the world. While having recruited as associates a few fellow patients during his long hospitalization, he was, in fact, the only full-time member of his organization, to which he was intensely devoted, endlessly writing plans of action illustrated with multiple allegoric pencil drawings in several notebooks he always carried with him. While he was quite adapted to the life at the psychiatric hospital, he voluntarily agreed to participate in the trial of this new medication and complied faithfully with the treatment. The medication, and perhaps, in part, the friendly attention he received from me rather than the anomy that otherwise surrounded him, accomplished the promise of its anti-delusional effect in a few weeks. However, as the whole belief system that had provided sense to his life during the previous ten to fifteen years began to fade away, that patient, joyous and energetic while involved in his "Organization of Talented People," became a despondent man who realistically evaluated his bleak, lonely, empty future—during his years of confinement he had lost whatever prior skills he had as a musician and lacked any family or extra-familial social support or any alternative passionate theme to provide meaning to his life. In turn, the institution that held him lacked any substantive discharge planning protocol or available social services that could orient him in terms of community resources and services. During my weekly visits to the asylum, I did my best to discuss possible activities he could explore once discharged but, not surprisingly, none of them could compete with the attractiveness that characterized his lost grandiose quest. Within a month, in despair, and still in the hospital but scheduled for discharge, he sliced his wrist veins and died overnight.

His ghost still visits me occasionally to remind me of the risks entailed in wanting more change than what the patient wants, in assuming that the elimination of a delusion is a blessing and not at times a curse, and in the crucial importance of counting on a steady social support during and after major life changes (not to mention the need to assure appropriate discharge planning and community aftercare for improving hospitalized patients).

Most initial therapeutic consultations have an explicit starting point, a statement that defines the sometimes agreed upon, sometimes competing reasons for the consultation, areas of conflict and expectations of change. In fact, most therapeutic *sessions* have a title, a theme—or perhaps I should state that I find it useful for my work to detect that title—or create it—on the basis of the first set of utterances or the first themes of that specific visit. It establishes the basis for the plot of the story we will be working with. Sometimes that title appears as an apparently irrelevant first comment—"I am tired today," "Seems that a storm is coming," "How are we today?" and so on.

We may agree or disagree with the formulations of the patients' goal, with the means by which they propose to achieve change, with the pace and sequence proposed, or with who should be involved in the process. We may even propose alternative goals that are more humble, broader or simply different, and these conversations may lead to new formulations, and may orient the patients toward deciding whether to continue working with us or not.

The relationship that therapists establish with their own guiding models affects their relationship with patients not only in terms of the orientation, style, and focus of the consultation but also in terms of competing hegemonies: the more faithful attention the therapists pay to their models, the less their flexibility in terms of accompanying patients in the exploration of their dilemmas. However, unless the therapists have guidelines for action, they will be hopelessly engulfed in the patients' story, with the risk of being only able to accompany them into their labyrinth without any conceptual Ariadne's thread that will allow them to exit from it.

These last statements are, of course, booby-trapped by constructionist recursivity: reality is always built through the lens of our assumptions and models, and there are no "patients" who hang out there, free from therapeutic constructs that organize and privilege what we perceive, nor "stories" that do not reside simultaneously in the storytellers and in all those who listen to them, therapists included.

In the course of a therapeutic consultation, we therapists may comfortably inhabit an amalgam of accompanying and guiding, of "being there," models, techniques, empathy styles, and our prior experience. Conceptual models and guidelines melt in the long run into our professional self, granting us certain coherence in our practice, with all of the pros and cons that are entailed. But on occasions we may invoke, as a lens, models or theories that are not incarnated into our professional self, with the hope that "looking" through their lens would add a clearer perspective or offer a new orientation and a pathway out of some entanglement, guiding our actions when our internal compass fails to orient us.[2]

In fact, it could be argued that, unless we therapists acquire a recursive awareness of the models we rely on, that is, a certain minimally detached, instrumental view of our theories, holding them as "theories" or "models," we may risk becoming their slaves, rather than their owners.

At the same time, we cannot *not* be at the mercy of our own personal style, esthetic preferences, and the potential bias generated by our prior teachers and our own life experiences. Hence, we should be at least aware of the multiple possible ways in which those extra-methodological variables express themselves in our clinical practice, increasing or decreasing our tolerance to a different range of emotions and our sensitivity to themes, conflicts, and their potential resolution, with a combination of magnifying glasses and blind spots that Mony Elkaim (1997) so aptly called "resonances."

This chapter focuses on nine sessions of family therapy that I facilitated a number of years ago, a treatment that taught me an important lesson on the subject of the focus and the endpoint of therapy. In this particular case, my own goals and expectations—conceptually reasonable but out of sync with what had been requested by the members of this family—once again exceeded those explicitly stated or even desired by them.

My first contact with this family was a telephone call from a woman who stated: "I am taking a course in family therapy at college. While studying the subject it became clear to me that my family needs family therapy, and I need some help because I am trapped in the middle, triangulated between my father and my brother. My brother has been suffering from chronic schizophrenia for many years and lives downtown, near your office. My father, who is already retired, lives abroad, and returned recently to take care of some family business and the rental of our family house. But he found my brother in such a terrible shape that he tried to rescue him by inviting him to live together for a short period while he was preparing the house for a new renter, and tried to teach him to take better care of himself, to cook a bit, to stay clean, those basic kinds of things. But now they are at each other's throats, driving each other crazy and driving me crazier. They phone me at any hour of the day or night and drag me from where I live, seventy miles or so away, to their house, sometimes in the middle of a snowstorm, because they are shouting at each other and ready to kill each other. Would you please see us as soon as possible? They already agreed that it would be a good idea."

I explored whether there were any other members of the nuclear family. She stated that the family was limited to the three, as her mother had died a few years ago and they don't have any extended family in the region. I checked my appointment book, and I asked her to invite the family for an interview a few days later, explaining that it would take place in a context where the interview would be observed from behind a one-way mirror by a small group of colleagues (at that time, that setting was my routine way of working with families, as part of a training intensive). She agreed and informed me that she would also explain that to her family—she assumed that they wouldn't mind.

They arrived punctually. The woman who made the phone call was a pleasant, friendly, energetic Anglo-Saxon in her mid-thirties, with long, frizzy hair, comfortable and slightly unconventional clothing, and an overall strong presence. Her brother, two years younger, displayed all of the stigmata of the "chronic schizophrenic patient in the community": he was disheveled, dressed with dirty and worn out clothes, rather disorganized in his behavior, and filled with mannerisms. Their father was an extremely elegant gentleman, with a strong British accent, very contained in his behavior and displayed many social graces.

(continued)

(continued)

*It was an unusual group: a Jane Goodall look-alike, Dustin Hoffman's charac-
ter from "Rain Man," and an "old English butler" in the style of some of the
best characterizations by Anthony Hopkins. I will call them by these names
throughout this chapter.*

Mr. Hopkins told me that he spent a good part of the year living in a small
guest house on a British Caribbean island, rather modestly, subsisting on his
retirement and the income from rental of their home in the United States,
and was also passing some money monthly to his son. Dustin lived in a local
halfway house near a community mental health center where he participated
on and off in outpatient programs and was followed in monthly contacts by
a psychiatrist. In addition to state disability and basic health insurance, he
acknowledged receiving a modest monthly support from his father. Jane lived
by herself—sometimes with her boyfriend—an hour away by car. Mr. Hopkins
repeats the story than Jane told me: he was currently in the area, and that
he visited periodically whenever he needed to find new tenants for the home
and to see how his son was doing. He explained that when he met Dustin this
time he found him in such a poor shape that he asked him to move in with
him temporarily, for a month or two, while he, Mr. Hopkins, reconditioned
the house for the next rental. His intention was "to patch Dustin up, buy
him some new clothes, teach him how to wash himself and how to cook,
and all that." However, they quickly found themselves locked in an unten-
able, damned-if-you-do-and-damned-if-you-don't type of constant fight—an
escalation of advices and refusals—that was driving everybody totally mad.
He sensed that he could not leave Dustin in his current condition, but his son
refused to shape up, and Mr. Hopkins felt that he could not just abandon
Dustin in such a poor state.

I explored their goals and expectations for the family consultation, and
they were able to articulate them rather clearly. Focused on their individual
needs, Jane wanted "out of all this, I need to go on with my own life. I don't
want to keep being caught in the middle. And I have to be able to travel for
some of my activities and cannot be trapped by all this." Mr. Hopkins, stated,
in turn, "I want to go back to my modest refuge in the Caribbean and to my
daily routines. I want to be able to disengage from my son, but cannot leave
him like this." And Dustin echoed a similar goal: "Me too, I want to be left
alone and go on with my life without so much meddling."

The absent fourth character in the family consultation was also introduced in the first session, and she acquired greater and greater presence in
subsequent encounters: "mother," who had died five years before, and was
described as having been, and continued being in spite of her demise, a
strong, intense, charismatic central character in everybody's life. Mr. Hopkins
described her as an enfant prodige, a remarkable mind and multifaceted

artist who had studied with renowned artists—Calder, Miro, among others—in her early twenties and, after having been spurned from an important exhibit, she impulsively married one of her suitors, Mr. Hopkins, a parks and landscape designer, and proceeded to live the rest of her life practically secluded in their house. She was portrayed by the three of them as an extremely temperamental and possessive woman who would spend months on end inside the house, painting, destroying her paintings and re-painting them, playing the piano with virtuosity, studying Chinese by herself until acquiring fluency but refusing any opportunity to travel to the Orient, and prone to tantrums and displays of despair—they described several episodes in which, sometimes triggered by a minor event, she would run up three flight of stairs to the attic, her hair flowing in trail (her hair reached the floor, as she never trimmed it), locking herself in it, and proceeding to wail in despair while banging the walls with her fists. The reciprocal agreement with her husband was clear: "The house is my territory," she was described as defining it explicitly, "and you take care of the garden." And he, obligingly, landscaped the garden into an almost medieval refuge, growing powerful hedges around the house that, over the years, totally hid the property from the street.

The couple had two offspring: Jane, a strong, rebellious, creative tomboy attached to her father, involved in outdoor adventures that evolved over the years into a commitment first to wildlife preservation in Africa and more recently to human rights advocacy; and Dustin, born two years later, clearly his mother's favorite, who was a mild, introspective child ("an expert in inner wilderness," commented his sister with tenderness, contrasting him from her own outdoor vocation) and an outstanding student with few friends who used to stay at home with his mother studying, accompanying her and writing poetry until he decided to go to college, where he promptly experienced a rather catastrophic psychotic breakdown that was diagnosed as schizophrenia. From then on he alternated between living at home under his mother's care and hospitalizations due to relapses. Seven years ago, the mother was diagnosed in turn with cancer. She refused treatment, and, as the disease progressed, she was eventually hospitalized for pain management and terminal care. Jane described this hospitalization as a dramatic period, with her mother, profoundly emaciated, moaning in pain, surrounded by intravenous lines and catheters of all kinds. She remembered in session a telling circumstance in which she, Jane, asked her mother's permission to cut her hair, that was endlessly entangled with the tubing, and the mother, while having nodded in agreement, looked with an expression of utter horror as her daughter carried out that task, which was necessary, but symbolically terminal for mother.[3] After her death, the remaining members of the family disbanded: Jane, who lived on her own since her late teens, continued with her activities, mostly abroad,

(continued)

(continued)

Dustin moved to a halfway community house for chronic psychiatric patients with the psychopharmacologic follow up taking place at a local community mental health center, and Mr. Hopkins retired and established residence in a small Caribbean island where he had apparently taken occasional refuge on prior occasions, escaping from the chaos at home.

The family described the physically absent but emotionally very present member—referred to as "Mother" by both offspring and as "Madame" by her widower—with vividness and enthusiasm, exchanging anecdotes and memories about her, interspersed with frequent laughter by the younger two and a controlled giggling by their father. In fact, that theme seemed to inject extreme animation in this otherwise rather subdued family. When, early in the treatment, I praised them for having been so faithful in keeping wife/mother so much alive in their midst, Mr. Hopkins answered rather pensively, "Ah, yes, yes, yes, the ancient cult of Madame!"

"Cult of Madame," indeed! They described, almost sacramentally, that the house had been carefully kept as it was when Madame was alive, a temple at the service of that cult: rooms were filled not only with the memory of her but also with her memorabilia. Since her death five years ago, a collection of her paintings and other objects d'art, as well as her piano and a substantial amount of sheet music, remained untouched and in the house, inventoried for purposes of rental agreements. A vignette: I asked "Have you ever considered donating the sheet music to the Music Department of the local college or her paintings to a local museum or something like that?" to which Mr. Hopkins answered very seriously "Oh, no, no! Madame wouldn't like that!" with both siblings nodding in agreement.

As the sessions progressed, I became more and more fascinated with the presence of that ghost during the consultation, as Madame was virtually materialized once and over again not only in the conversation but also throughout the interaction. For instance, while the daughter usually sat in a corner of the room, father and son would tend to sit in a row, leaving a space or an empty chair between them, and they would frequently lean forward to converse, as if Madame would be sitting between them, reproducing her central role in the stable triangulation that seemed to have operated in the family throughout their life. On one of these occasions in which the sitting arrangement would include an empty space between them, I moved an empty chair toward that space, defining it as Madame's chair, and everybody interacted around this virtual scene with excitement and ease. Dustin even sat momentarily in that chair and imitated her, to everybody's amusement.

A powerful, if omnipotent, fantasy started to take form in me over several sessions: if I would be able to exorcise this ghost, if I could help them dissolve the "Ancient Cult of Madame" as a dominant theme, this family would be able to evolve, family members would be able to relate with one another in a different manner—and, further, perhaps Dustin would be able to free himself from the trap of schizophrenia.

Consequently, in what I considered to be an appropriate moment during the sixth session, I pushed the issue further in the midst of still another conversation about Madame: "Perhaps, as we are nearing Memorial Day, a day in which one honors those already dead, it would be a respectful time to let go of Madame's ghost. Where is she buried?" Jane informed me—in a another long anecdote filled with humor—that her mother didn't have any burial site but was "all around us," as she had been cremated and her ashes scattered into the wind from an airplane over the area. The rather macabre and very symbolic story of the difficult attempts at disposing of Madame's ashes from a small plane, with the wind blowing them back into the cockpit and her struggling to find a way to block it from doing that, was told by Jane in an extremely jovial manner, while the rest of the family echoed it with laughter. I insisted, "Well, in spite of Madame's insistence in remaining among us, could you think of a place nearby that could take the place of, and represent her burial site, one around which you all would be able to organize for her the rituals one develops to render homage to those dead?"

At that moment Dustin, who, until then, always intervened in a very flaky or timid fashion or would leave the office whenever he experienced some tension, leaned forward and, looking at me intently while pointing at me with his index finger, admonished me sternly and with a firm voice: "Sluzki! Not one word more! This is going too far! This family cannot tolerate it! Change the conversation into trivial subjects and don't talk any longer about all this!"

I was startled by his intensity and his clarity. I also became slightly physically afraid—I remember wondering whether some of the colleagues who were observing the interaction behind the one-way mirror would enter the office and help me if Dustin physically attacked me. As the tension subsided, I remember evoking, but contrasting, my old asylum patient and thinking that, if the "Ancient Cult of Madame" would be completely eliminated, would that not imply a loss of meaning and of purpose, of a reason for being in the world for Dustin and perhaps also for the other two long-standing priests and priestess of the Ancient Cult of Madame? I also reminded myself of the very specific goals posed by each of them during the first session, namely, for Mr. Hopkins, to be able to return to his Caribbean routine, for Jane to be able to disengage, and for Dustin to be able to live a reasonably content life the way he had been doing it, regardless of the fact that others—sister, father, and myself—didn't consider it ideal.

This cascade of emotions and thought took place in the course of seconds, and led me to agree explicitly with Dustin's request. Jane asked her brother,

(continued)

(continued)

as if requesting permission, "But couldn't I go on with my own need to bury mother?" to which I answered in his stead, "You may do that, but I will respect Dustin's request not to go on with this theme at this time." Mr. Hopkins, always placating and a bit startled himself, agreed immediately with dropping the theme. And I proceeded, during the rest of that session and in the following three, to focus on "trivial subjects," namely the specific ways in which their original goals could be met, including pragmatic arrangements, money disbursements, timing of their moves, living arrangements for Dustin that would be satisfactory to all, and issues of autonomy and connectedness between the three. The banned theme was not touched at all throughout that timespan, except for a comment by Jane at the end of eighth session, to the effect that the theme of needing a symbolic burial place for her mother had been extremely moving and useful for her, a comment that was clearly addressed to me as an expression of appreciation.

At the ninth and last session, Jane expressed her enormous relief for having ceased becoming an arbiter for conflicts between father and brother for at least the past two months. In turn, Mr. Hopkins informed me that he had found a tenant for his house and was ready to return to his Caribbean refuge. Dustin stated that he was also ready to return to living by himself—in better living quarters as well as more satisfactory mechanisms for receiving his modest monthly allowance that had been agreed upon with active and effective participation of his father, Dustin himself, and his caseworker.

Mr. Hopkins surprised us all in that last session with a brilliant initiative that provided Dustin with a new, coveted identity, namely, that of being a poet, which had been a more private, family-based alternative persona of Dustin. It happened that Dustin had been writing and kept as valuable property in a binder a number of his poems, most of them short, Koan-like pieces. A few weeks before this last session, Mr. Hopkins asked his son to lend him that binder and proceeded to produce with them a private limited edition of one hundred copies of Collected Poems of Dustin Hoffman, which he gave to his son as a present near the end of the last session, thus legitimizing his identity as a poet. The session and the therapy ended with reciprocal expressions of appreciation between all of us.

What a fascinating and moving intervention-in-action was entailed in Mr. Hopkins' gesture, that of shifting the harsh narrative of the son as psychotic to the more benevolent and attractive one of the son as an eccentric bohemian poet! As a pure speculation, perhaps Madame, an art-oriented person, fostered that identity in the past while Mr. Hopkins, an outdoor individual, disqualified it, and that new gesture imbued the value of symbolic reconnection between father and son, bypassing (but using the language of) Madame.

I was able to follow up this family for three years through occasional friendly phone calls to or from Jane or Mr. Hopkins. Jane married her long-time boyfriend, who joined her in her life project as an expat human rights worker in Africa. Dustin maintained his rather marginal lifestyle (even though, according to his sister, in a less disorganized way) but was also socializing on and off with groups of reference that were not pathology- but literary-based, mainly in a bookstore-literary café where local poets would meet on a weekly basis for an evening of poetry reading. Mr. Hopkins continued his low-key bucolic life at his Caribbean retreat. And as for me, if I did inhale a speck of those ashes of Madame's body that had been cast into the wind a few years before above the area where my office happened to be, I am glad to report that it didn't seem to have had any manifestation that I could notice, beyond fond memories toward her family.

Discussion

This treatment course entailed for me several major learning experiences. It became not only a lesson in humility but a reminder that, while exploring dominant narratives and evolving some of them with the family that consults, it is important to keep in mind their explicitly stated goals and to attempt to discriminate whether some therapeutic agendas may follow our, and not their, expectations.[4] This clash, I might add, may be at the core of the comfortable notion of "resistance," frequently used as a pseudo-explanation—what Gregory Bateson (1972) called "dormitive principles"—slapped on the individual, couple, or family who consults us but does not change according to our goals and expectations, that is, according to the mandates of whatever model or assumptions that guided us in the course of their therapy (Sluzki, 1983).

There are many caveats to this discussion. Perhaps Dustin's reaction of blocking my proposal simply indicated that I made an error in pace, as I should have followed, rather than led, the proposal to bury Madame, if and when that theme appeared in the course of the treatment—somehow I thought it did at that time, but evidence showed me otherwise. Perhaps my impatience led me to bypass intermediate steps in the process of accompanying them in the transformation of their story. Perhaps I had detected Jane's readiness to move on and was not sensitive enough to consider that the proposal risked destabilizing the position of her brother as the main priest of that cult. Or perhaps there was something soothing, something familiar, for them in the "Ancient Cult of Madame," considering all the liveliness, joviality, teasing, and frequent laughter evoked by their management of the ghostly presence of Madame, and the idea of a burial place would rob them of the remnants of the family glue that Madame's omnipresence may have provided.

One way or another, the fact remains that I became fascinated by the virtual presence of Madame in this family and allured by the stories and the rituals that held that presence in place. I joined, in that fashion, this family's "psychotic game," in the systemic self-organizing sense alluded to by Selvini Palazzoli, Cirillo, Selvini, and Sorrentino (1989) in their proposal of that notion. In fact, any family story originally offered and sustained by a family who consults becomes, as therapy evolves, an evolving narrative that ends up "inhabiting" us all, that is, sustained by the larger therapist–family system. However, the more we therapists become trapped by our attraction to the content of the story (the tattle-tale of this may be our mesmerized fascination for it), the more difficult it will become to remain open to therapeutic means of gently destabilizing it. Interestingly, Cecchin's wise plea toward *curiosity* (Cecchin, 1987; Cecchin, Lane, & Ray, 1994) embeds both the recommendation to remain empathic and connected with people and themes and the caution to avoid becoming too fascinated by that story. This double injunction aims at facilitating the destabilization of the original narrative through challenging current and exploring new views and different explanatory models while not moving ahead of the family in the readiness to engage in alternative scenarios. In a duet with the ethereal presence of the patient whom I mentioned at the beginning of this chapter, who whispers to me "Don't want more than what a patient wants," the friendly ghost of Gianfranco Cecchin also visits me with certain frequency to remind me, with a warm smile, of his admonition "Don't fall in love with a story." A tall order indeed.

At another level of analysis and of musing, the three live actors of this consultation had practically no shared personal social network, as they lived at considerable distance from each other and with different orbits of interests and of activities and contacts. Their central knot and common link may have been Madame. Keeping Madame's sanctuary—the house that was being rented and that gave reason for them to get together every so often—assured their connectedness, as it allowed them to enact every so often the rituals of the "Ancient Cult of Madame," as Mr. Hopkins aptly named it.

Was that the reason for Dustin's strong objection to the suggestion of symbolically burying Madame? Or was it that establishing a locus for her soul would make her, or her death, too real? But there I go, falling again in love with the story.

Notes

1 That diagnosis, practically out of use in present times (and absent both from the DSM-IVR and the ICD-10), was created by the German psychiatrist Karl Kahlbaum in 1863 and revived by Emil Kraepelin in 1913 in reference to adults who displayed a systematized monothematic delusional system without deterioration in other cognitive or emotional spheres. Adults with this presentation would either become charismatic leaders of sects, cults, or countries, or, if unsuccessful, be diagnosed as suffering from this form of "atypical psychosis" (or both!).

2 These are frequently one or another of the "multiple voices" that Salvador Minuchin (1987) and so many of us therapists recognize as materializing though our actions in the course of our own practice.

3 I highlight this episode not only because of its poignancy but also because, in the course of the nine sessions of this family treatment, Jane wore her hair shoulder-long and rather wild during the first three sessions, then cut her hair twice, trimming it substantially on one occasion, to later doing it again, appearing with her hair cut quite short (both reasonable due to her plans to return to her activities in a refugee camp in Africa and to her progressive differentiation from her mother-surrogate role).

4 Not that both agendas necessarily differ. Even further, there are therapists known for their special focus (such as detaching, or solving conflicts with, family of origin; feminism and male oppression; prolonged or problematized mourning; sexual identity and coming out; re-entry from cults; sexuality, or cross-cultural clashes in the couple), and families are frequently referred to them, or select them, precisely for that emphasis, and they may even complain if the therapist deviates from that thematic frame.

The Naming: The Awakening of Two Ghost Children   6

When, in the course of therapy, we establish a bridge between a dramatic event lodged in the past and an apparently disconnected problem or symptom of the present that lead to a consultation, we may witness on occasions one of those well-known "Aha!" moments, the emotional and associative reverberations of a new fit. That "click" would be usually defined (at least by us, therapists with a psychodynamic background) as "a moment of insight," of illuminated enrichment or reorganization of the story into a meaningful narrative that ties past and present as well as present and future, and that is both esthetically pleasing and liberating. Problems or symptoms that were previously experienced as senseless or random acquire a symbolic fit and are incorporated into a sensible plot with plausible explanatory assumptions, and not infrequently fade away. Therapy is, in that sense, a transformation of a dominant story into another one that opens doors, provides sense, and exorcises pathology.

In fact, in the practice of therapy—be it individual, couples or family-based—therapists routinely highlight, comment, intertwine and braid (Cobb, 2013b) information that in the original problem-based narrative appeared as secondary if not disconnected or even omitted from the core plot, such as additional historic, chronologic, cultural or other contextual data about characters and/or setting. Throughout therapy many ghosts that are hidden and seemingly forgotten from the past revive, acquiring roles that become sometimes protagonic, frequently benign, and even magical. And when those that are present in a disjointed, malignant way (as in the case of many PTSD syndrome-like flashbacks, or, for that matter, those visiting the family, as the scenario presented in Chapter 3) are named, their materialization makes them lose power, after which they can be tamed if not expelled.

The destabilization and ulterior transformation of the problem-saturated story requires an active exploratory involvement by the interviewer—a probing that, while conceptually grounded in rather sophisticated epistemologies, has all the appearance of being "naïve." In this regard, a rich interviewing "technology" has been developed and thoroughly discussed in the systemic/narrative literature, including, but not limited to, positive connotations, circular questions of a different kind (Selvini, Boscolo, Cecchin, & Prata, 1980; Tomm, 1987, 1988), the above-mentioned epistemological "curiosity" (Cecchin, 1987), and externalizing explorations (White, 1984; White & Epston, 1990).[1]

In many occasions the patients—be they individuals, couples or families— readily provide, by omission or commission, information about a multitude of characters, events, and circumstances of their life that appear not to be weaved into the complex tapestry of their narrative. Enriching their core narratives by establishing bridges that connect those pieces to other events illuminate new perspectives, new explanatory principles, new views, and new ethical corollaries that transform the prior problem-based narrative.

Fortunately, there are happy circumstances in which it takes the therapist only to formulate a couple of well-placed reasonable questions to trigger a narrative transformation.

The following consultation provides an example of what we are talking about, enriched by a spontaneously enacted ritual that reaffirmed and anchored the transformed story.

The initial interview with this couple in their mid-thirties, of low socio-economic origins but successfully ascending in that ladder, takes place in a family therapy-oriented sliding-scale private clinic in a Santiago, Chile, where I was providing consultations as part of a training program on family therapy for its personnel. The interview, conducted in Spanish, was observed from behind a one-way mirror by a team of professionals from that center—the consulting couple had been informed that that was the routine intake procedure in that clinic and accepted being observed. The appointment was prompted by a man who explained during the initial telephone call that he was following the recommendation of his wife's psychiatrist, who was treating her because of an increasingly severe puerperal (i.e., post-partum) depression.

The couple arrives at the appointed time. I invite them in from the waiting room while reminding them that, unless they objected, we would be observed by a few colleagues from behind a one-way mirror. I also tell them that, if they agreed, during the last part of the interview I may ask that team to offer us whatever comments they would find appropriate about the consultation, to further enrich the process. Again, they accept.

The latter follows the modality of the "reflective team" (Andersen, 1991) already discussed elsewhere in this book—an extremely powerful methodology to create a witnessing community as a way of helping to anchor changes that may have occurred during the consultation.

Both appear to be in their early thirties, are socially pleasant throughout the consultation, well connected with me and tender with each other. Marcos, formally attired with jacket and tie, displays an efficient "in charge" modality. Luisa, in turn, shows a more subdued attitude but becomes more animated as the interview progresses. He opens the consultation informing me that they were referred to that clinic in order to open new means of treatment for his wife, who has been increasingly depressed since the delivery of their daughter, some two years ago. Currently, she is is barely able to deal with the daily chores related to the care of their child, and unable to even contemplate the idea of returning to her previous job, an activity that she not only used to enjoy but also constituted a healthy contribution to the family budget. Luisa, smiling sadly, agrees with his description, stating that she doesn't understand what is happening with her, as her lack of energy and enthusiasm is the opposite of the optimistic and positive style that characterized all her previous life. She provides a detailed litany of symptoms to show how depression expressed itself in her. Marcos adds that Luisa had been diagnosed as suffering from post-partum depression by a competent psychiatrist specialized in psychopharmacology who prescribed her antidepressant medication. She has tried several medications without any success, even in reasonably high doses, and her psychiatrist has finally suggested that they try some "talking therapy."

Their mode of delivery is pleasant and harmonious. They follow a style known as "conversational duet" (Falk, 1980), namely, their narrative being composed by the successive contribution of each of them, "sharing the microphone" rather than competing for it, sometimes one of them beginning a sentence and the other completing it without tension or obfuscation.

I ask them whether they would mind if I probe into their personal and relational history. They agree, and I begin to do so. Marcos describes, with low-key pride, his very humble origins—low-wage working uneducated parents, many siblings—and his professional evolution from full-time "gofer" at age 14 at a central drug store/pharmacy to manager of that establishment, in spite of his own low level of formal education. Luisa, in turn, states that her family was a bit better to do than Marcos's, as her parents finished elementary school. She in turn finished high school and has been working as a salesperson at a local department store—a job she liked—until quite advanced in her recent pregnancy. They then conjointly describe their relational history, including three years of gratifying courtship, that received the emotional approval from both their families of origin, and leading to six years of congenial and reciprocally supportive marriage.

Marcos adds that their relationship has been further strengthened by what they label the most traumatic experience in their life, the birth four years ago of a full-term baby who died a few hours after delivery due to a severe congenital abnormality. Luisa comments that she had been informed beforehand by her obstetrician that the baby appeared to be anencephalic, but the information came at an advanced stage of pregnancy, so she didn't have any choice but to proceed with the pregnancy and deliver the newborn, knowing that it would not survive.

They provide this information in a low tone but quite matter-of-factly, while I echo these exchanges with rather expressive compassionate comments— contributing my emotions to what I sensed was an unusually flat delivery of that poignant narrative.

They respond to my empathic statements with every-day-life philosophical truisms. They went on to comment that their families of origin had been a source of additional important support during that ordeal. They were going to go on by describing who was whom in their families, but I interrupted that line of thought and ask them—still in an empathic tone of voice that informed that I remained lodged in that emotional climate—whether it was a girl or a boy. She states that it was a boy. I then ask them what was his name.

They both react with shock to my question, looking at each other as if they wouldn't have understood what I said—or if I wasn't understanding their story. Then, acting as if I would have asked an inappropriate or dumb question, they explain, using an almost patronizing tone, that the baby didn't have a name because he had died at birth, as they knew that would happen, as they had explained. I answer that I understood all that, but what I wanted to know was the name they had chosen for the baby before the information about his non-viability late in the pregnancy. After a brief silence, some hesitation and a carefully crafted exchange of gazes between them that signals to me that we are dealing with a delicate subject, he answers that the name they had originally chosen for that baby was "Lucas." I then ask them where Lucas was buried.

Again they seem flabbergasted: "Nowhere," he answers, "because the baby had been 'disposed of' by the hospital with our consent—with my consent at the moment," Marcos clarifies, "as Luisa was too distressed by the

(continued)

(continued)

whole situation to be able to discuss the issue." Luisa comments in turn that, in fact, she hadn't even wanted to see him, while Marcos adds that that had been also the recommendation of the obstetrician at the maternity clinic, given the deformities of the baby. They comment that it took her several months to recover from that terrible experience, while he had to deal with all the practicalities of life and also continue with his job, so he had to pull himself out of his own distress just to go on, and to be able to support her. In the long run, they say, they both were able to take that blow as one of those awful things that just happen in life. Within a year, they continue, they decided to try again and she became pregnant, in part "to help them fill the void," following the suggestion of well-wishing relatives as well as that of the obstetrician, in addition to their own desire to have a child. However, after the birth of that second child, a girl named Gloria (they are quick to add her name signaling the impact of our prior exchange), Luisa became increasingly depressed.

I praise them both for their capacity to be together with tenderness during those terrible periods of pain and loss, and Marcos for his fortitude (it was clear to me that that was an important value for him). I then asked Marcos how his own health has been during all this, adding that even Atlas may have had some muscle pains while carrying the world on his shoulders. She concurs and praises his resilience. Marcos states that he has been always a very healthy person, adding as in passing—after commenting that he is not a complaining person, but as I asked . . .—that recently, in the past few weeks, he has been sleeping poorly. I ask him whether he believes there is any reason for that, and he comments that, in addition to his concern for Luisa, he has been bothered by nightmares, more specifically a recurrent dream about Pedro, a brother two years his junior who had died of diphtheria during childhood. As a consequence of these scary dreams, in which his brother appears as a ghost in the distance, he has been haunted by memories of the death and the wake of his brother, a subject he had completely forgotten for decades. I ask Marcos how old was his brother Pedro when he died. He answers that he died when he was four. I then ask him how old Lucas would be if he were alive today.

Marcos looks at me with total amazement, answers "Four," and begins to cry intensely, while protesting in-between bursts of sobbing and with a strangled voice that he cannot believe what is going on with him, that he had never cried before except during the first hours after the birth and death of the then unnamed child. Luisa, tearful and tenderly, holds his hand and caresses him in consolation. I, also quite moved by the process, and after we calm down a bit, "welcome" him back "after four years of absence," praising him for having delayed his own pain all these years in order to protect Luisa, praising his brother Pedro for having helped him bring forth the issue, and stating that the time seemed to have arrived for her to console him for his share of their loss and pain, necessary to be able to fully welcome Gloria to their world. An almost sacred silence ensues, while they hold hands and calm down.

At that time, and after a short prelude in which I told them that I was thinking of offering a voice to the other witnesses of our conversation, and after obtaining again their consent to do it, I invited the colleagues behind the one-way mirror to turn on the light of their cubicle, revert the sound system, and offer any witnessing comments they may consider useful for us.[2] They do so, and offer rather subdued and at times emotional comments, as they have been themselves quite moved by the course of the events, as well as caring (and carefully crafted) comments, mainly echoing my own statements of praise for their reciprocal support during their ordeal.

I thank the team for their comments, and ask the couple whether they had in turn any reaction to their observations. They thank them in turn. I proceed to end that interview, telling them that they probably have enough issues to process after our conversation, and expressing again my appreciation for their openness and their mutual support that allowed for these difficult themes to be opened. I also offered them to continue this conversation within a week, if they wished. They agree and, after specifying the day and hour of the next appointment, they leave a bit in a daze while I return to discuss the interview with the observing team—the team's main question, posed in different ways, was "How did you know?" and, truthfully, I answered that I didn't, that I just asked those questions because they were reasonable—and absent from their story. In regard to the question about the age of his brother at the time of his death, I told them that I believe in the wisdom of the unconscious and in the power of the dreams as well as in the esthetic principle that governs narratives.

In a follow-up consultation a few days later the couple describes a series of conversations between them in which each blamed their own self for not having been more sensitive and taken better care of the other, in each occasion being rebutted by the other, in an escalation of self-flagellation and reciprocal appreciation. Luisa appears clearly animated and comments that somehow she feels more energetic and in better mood. Marcos in turn tells me that a few days after the previous session, and following an impulse, he went by himself to the town's cemetery to visit the burial site of his brother Peter, an act that he hasn't done for years, and ended up crying for both Peter and Lucas. He jokingly adds that he told Luisa that that debunks the myth that he is the strong one in the family. She comments in turn that she told him, and they agreed, that the next time he goes to the cemetery to visit Peter's tomb she would go with him "because, thanks to what he did, it is as if Lucas would be also buried there."

(continued)

(continued)

I praise them again for their capacity to be a strong resource for one other and for having transformed a ghost that was haunting them into a tender and sad memory that they can live with. They agree with this formulation with a tearful smile.

The themes touched during the rest of the second interview included Louisa's project to return to work the following week, as her mother had offered them to take care of their daughter for a few hours every day, and other practical subjects that placed me mainly as a witness of their fluid decision-making. I close the session expressing of my pleasure for having been able to have such a rich conversation with them, adding that, should the need arise, there would be colleagues in the clinic able and ready to accompany them in further explorations. In turn, they express their appreciation for the help they received.

Was this transformation the product of their having been open to resonate with a pair of well-placed, almost obvious, questions triggered by the clinical acumen of a therapist with many years of experience? Was it simply the right moment in the balance of their relationship that allowed him to uncork bottled-up emotions, making the first consultation one of those blessed opportunities that allows us to simply accompany our patients into a space of reflection while they themselves enrich their own story? Was it the result of providing to a (culturally enforced) manly man the opportunity and almost permission to break his stereotype and reach into painful suppressed emotions and memories? Was Luisa's depression a heroic overload of a shared sadness that her husband was unable to feel or express? Was it (also) a product of my belief in the importance of rituals—naming, wakes, burying, among many others—as we traverse markers both normative and circumstantial throughout life?

Many chronic interpersonal problems or personal symptoms seem only loosely attached from whatever temporary difficulty or painful event within the ups and downs of a life narrative that may have triggered them. To re-establish that connection is frequently the therapeutic orientation of therapists who use as a compass the assumption that many symptoms and conflicts derive from complicated bereavement or incomplete mourning related to (frequently traumatic) losses (e.g., Paul & Grosser, 1965; Paul, 1986; McGoldrick & Walsh, 2004). It merits noting that a constructivist reformulation of this orientation would be that traumatic losses can become "powerful attractors" (Sluzki, 1998b) that, when brought forth in the therapeutic conversation, allow for a transformation from a symptom-based narrative into one where the dominant feature is that loss.

The so-called symptom becomes then a reasonable (rather than aleatory), if secondary (rather than dominant), trait derived from it. The new story—which provides a reasonable context for emotions that until then appeared only as symptoms—can be further anchored with the prescription of appropriate rituals of homage to and reconciliation with the dead, and of letting go—acts that also further marginalize and frequently dissolve (rather than resolve) the previous conflicts or symptoms.

In sum, when we allow for a connection to be established between the presenting problem and a meaningful component of the patient/family's context, a richer if not alternative story may unfold (as is the case with the couple we have presented above), one that is more complex, textured, and flexible. This transformed story allows for a more resourceful management of the problem/symptom, as well as for a loss of centrality of the presenting symptoms or problems, until they fade away as something belonging to the past. The richer the interface we establish between participants and context, the greater the potential to generate different, better-formed stories, and/or for a shift of boundaries between dominant stories and other, novel ones. By altering the dominant theme in stories, or the dominance of one story over others, an increased range of ideas, emotions, and actions become available for the patient, the family, the therapist, and others involved. These shifts then generate a variety of different, new, frequently reparative acts. Hence, when the stories told by patients are meager in context or in characters, the therapist actively elicits richer descriptions. In addition, the therapist prefers descriptions of relationships that are cooperative rather than competitive—this applies not only to interpersonal relationships but also to relationships with events and even with symptoms (Fisch, Weakland, & Segal, 1982; de Shazer, 1985; Furman & Ahola, 1992). The relationship between the individual and the context may also be oriented to favor stories in which the location of the problem is externalized and dissociated from the self (as proposed by White, 1984; see also Tomm, 1989; White & Epston, 1990).

Needless to say, the opposite may be the case: Some problem-saturated stories are intertwined with, and supported by, nodal points of the patient/family's history. In turn, the facilitation of better-formed stories may question and destabilize, in fact, that connectedness, especially when these events are causally inscribed into problem-based narratives. Without disavowing the legitimacy of its components, the chronology may be questioned or altered, altering substantively the story's binding ethics. Such is the case of, for instance, a shared story of family conflicts leading to a schizophrenic manifestation in a family member, that can be transformed into one in which that very manifestation is a source of family stress and conflicts, hence shifting the narrative from a blame-generating assumption of family-induced mental illness to a description of relentless, strain-inducing efforts at dealing in a sane way with challenging thoughts and behaviors in its members.[3]

Three months later, at my request, the clinic made a follow-up phone call to the couple's household. Luisa answered, and informed that she is back to work part time, that she is feeling "herself" again, and that both she and Marcos are very appreciative for the experience of the consultation, that, as she put it, changed their lives.

Notes

1 These exploratory modalities are not the end but the means to destabilize the problem-saturated story. Transformative conversation often includes other components (Sluzki, 1992a, 1992b).

2 That small team joined me beforehand and I discussed with them the conceptual principles as well as the procedure and behavioral expectations for the members of a "reflecting team," following the guidelines recommended by the creator of that approach, that leans on the resonance of the witness as a powerful anchor for potential changes (Andersen, 1991). As is frequently the case with colleagues involved in that type of reflexive setting for the first time, they were mainly praising but sparse in their comments. In turn, the couple were happy to be seen by them in such an affirming light.

3 This is also one of the most likely impacts of psychoeducational approaches to severe psychiatric disorders (McFarlane, Dixon, Lukens, & Lucksted, 2007; Weber-Rouget & Aubry, 2007, among others) that usually result in reducing expectations, criticism, and high expressivity of negative emotions in the families of those patients, that in turn has the effect of reducing symptom and crisis in those individuals, which in turn . . .

Saudades at the Edge of the Self and the Merits of "Portable Families"

Many if not most people who have lost loved ones describe a similar experience following their loss: "I sensed that they were still there, that they never left, or that they had returned." Sometimes it limits itself to a faint hallucination of their voice, or hearing their characteristic footsteps in the house, smelling a whiff of their preferred perfume, hearing the jangling of their door keys, "almost" seeing them. Sometimes it is more than that.

A word that comes to my mind when trying to identify the feeling that accompanies or perhaps triggers those sensorial experiences in their many nuances is the idiosyncratic and rather untranslatable Portuguese word *saudade*, derived from the Latin *solitatem*, loneliness, and defined as "a feeling of nostalgic remembrance of people or things, absent or forever lost, accompanied by the desire to see or possess them once more" (Correia da Cunha, 1982). It evokes the sense of incompleteness that may have accompanied both the Portuguese navigators when spending long years of sailing the high seas—conquering and looting here and there—away from their homes and families who awaited them without the certainty of a re-encounter and the mirror-like experiences of their wives and families, wondering whether they would embrace them again. *Saudade* has both a hopeful and a fatalistic overtone: the object of longing—a loved one, home, our friends and family—is gone, is out of reach, but might return in a distant future—or not. No wonder it is a staple word in the lyrics of the *fados*, those famous melancholic Portuguese folkloric songs.

The passage of time may also be a kind and relentless healer: as the traumatic loss recedes in time, so usually does the daily imposing presence of the absence.

One day we discover that we haven't been tortured by that feeling of distress for several hours, or that we laughed with abandonment at something funny—a discovery that may flood us with guilt, as if that moment of joy or of involvement in our daily living would have affronted or betrayed the object of our sorrow or, even worst, expressed our joy of being alive. But that betrayal repeats itself until we realize that we may be able to live a life with at least a modicum of happiness while carrying within us that *saudade*, a permanent functional split of the self that may give us the authorization to re-engage into our capacity for joy and creativity—without forgetting.[1]

The more skin-bound the construction of the self favored by our culture, the more it will force us to distinguish between whomever we long for and wish to hear, see, touch, and embrace again, and the vacuum of his or her absence, discriminating, ultimately between self and the other. The Spartan dictum of a culture that informs us that we are skin-bounded individuals, that the others are "out there" and not part of our self, also instructs us to let go of whatever we cannot retain and continue with our life. This injunction will be counter-intuitive to, and clash with, the softer injunction emanating from cultures that define our self as enveloping others within its perimeter, that give us permission to rebel against our letting go of the departed—or those who will soon depart—by somehow retaining them with, or within, us.

The following clinical case will illustrate this alternative, culture-supported approach to loss and some consequences of its cross-cultural transplant and clash.

A few years ago, while doing some work at a psychiatric outpatient clinic for low-income patients within a general hospital in California, I was asked to see a 70-year-old bilingual Hispanic (a broad category encompassing people of Latin American origin living in the United States) woman, a well-known patient at that clinic. She had been in treatment for the past two years with a colleague, who asked me to take over her care as a patient arguing that, due to my bilingualism and multiculturalism, I would be better able to connect with her and figure out ways to treat her without falling into the frequent clashes that he himself experienced with that patient. He also informed me that this lady, whose improbable first name was Samotracia,[2] carried a diagnosis of atypical chronic schizophrenia. However, he added, her symptoms were quite impervious to the neuroleptic medication that he had prescribed for her already several months prior.

I accepted the referral. At the appointed time, this rather voluminous Mexican-born woman entered, her appearance marked by Mayan (or, broadly speaking, Mexican ancestral natives) facial features, long white hair combed into a bun, and a strong and coarse smoky voice. She dragged herself into my office with some huffing and puffing, greeting me in a respectful but not deferent stance, shifting to Spanish as soon as I indicated my fluency in that language.

For me, or perhaps for both of us, it was, so to speak, empathy at first sight. In fact, she reminded me immediately of the rotund and tender aboriginal woman depicted in a mother-and-child engraving by Clement Moreau titled Madonna Guaraní that decorated a wall in my home since childhood.[3]

In order to allow my own biases to develop rather than incorporating those of my more biologically oriented colleague, I chose not to read her rather thick clinical folder prior to the consultation. So, after the first social graces, I proposed to her to start from scratch: "I haven't read the previous notes on your chart. I may do it later, but, to begin from a fresh place: in what way, if any, can I be of help?"

Samotracia began by listing in detail a litany of physical problems and symptoms, from a heart condition to her high blood pressure to a lingering fatigue; the latter was probably a combined effect of heart insufficiency, heart medications, and the frequent extra-pyramidal effects of the neuroleptics she had been prescribed. Her daily life followed a rather tight routine. Its highlights were daily walks in her neighborhood, some social life with neighbors, frequent contact with her daughters, and visits to various health care practitioners. Her diet was balanced, she didn't drink alcohol, and she took reasonably good care of her health, aside from her lack of interest in reducing her excessive weight. She was followed medically due to heart disease, which was reasonably well controlled with medication, and psychiatrically for what she called "nerves," a rather blanket diagnostic category frequently used by Latinos to encompass a variety of pains and aches of the soul. She would smoke one cigarette after each meal and was not ready to let that habit go, as it was, "one of the few pleasures I still can indulge in." After she exhausted her rosary of symptoms and provided a sketchy description of her current context, Samotracia began to unfold her story, not as a coherent stream, as it may appear in the narrative that follows, but as a series of anecdotes delivered in the course of many subsequent appointments. I saw her once every two weeks for an hour over approximately a year and a half.

She was born and raised in a very small, tight-knit countryside village in Mexico. Her parents were poor farmers, who scarcely knew how to read and write, and who were rather severe but inconsistent disciplinarians; Samotracia described being frequently beaten with a belt during childhood for one thing or another, as most children did in her neighborhood. At the same time, she described them as reasonably caring, while she portrayed herself as a rather wild adolescent who escaped from home as soon as she was legally able, married very young and shortly afterwards entered the

(continued)

(continued)

United States illegally together with her husband. Both worked as braceros, *itinerant hired laborers in different harvests, wandering from job to job until they settled in an agricultural region of California where they were able to legalize their status as permanent residents. They had four children. She had to work hard to make ends meet while raising her offspring, especially after she separated from her husband, a man whom she described as an alcoholic who was physically violent with her and their children during his weekend binges. She continued a life of sacrifice, raising her children while working steadily as a house cleaner until her body informed her that her workload was becoming too heavy and her heart began to decompensate clinically. As a consequence, with her children already launched with mixed success, she had to cease working. With her carefully managed meager social security income, some minimal savings, and the occasional economic help from her two daughters, she had lived for the past eight years in a small but pleasant two-room rented apartment that was open to a forest and located in a safe neighborhood not too distant from the clinic. As mentioned above, she had four offspring, two males and two females. Both sons had died years ago: one was killed in a gang-related shootout in east Los Angeles during late adolescence and the other, a homosexual musician, died of AIDS at age 33. The two daughters were alive. The oldest, an accountant with a mid-management job in a local firm, lived with her boyfriend in the same city as her mother. The youngest, a police officer, was married, doing well in her career, and lived with her family in a town several hours away by car from Samotracia. Both daughters maintained frequent phone contact with their mother. The daughter living nearby had dinner with her mother once a week, exchanged phone calls frequently, and was available for emergencies, although she carefully avoided interfering with her mother's treasured autonomy. The only other family member with whom Samotracia had any contact was a sister who lived in a city located on the east coast of the United States, and with whom she maintained rather frequent phone contact. She had a meager informal social network consisting of several acquaintances and neighbors, but no intimate friends.[4]*

I explored whether she had any religious practices and she told me that she had been raised Catholic but did not attend religious services. However, she prayed occasionally on her own as she believed in the afterlife in a rather undefined way. She joked that some of her other beliefs, such as brujerias, *were more in tune with her remote origins than with any organized religion.*

I couldn't agree more about that assertion, especially when Samotracia confided in me, after I gained some of her trust, that her two dead sons visited her rather frequently. In fact, since a number of years ago her sons would appear three or four times a week during the evening after dinner while she was reading or watching television. She explained to me that the first time one of them appeared to her she was terrified, but slowly she became used to these presences and, in fact, since then she enjoys them immensely. The one who visits her most frequently was the musician, whom, she confessed in a secretive voice, had been her favorite. During those visits they would converse and joke with her and reassure her that they were all right. Sometimes they would engage in minor mischief just to make her laugh by "monkeying around." They could even be a bit annoying and distracting at times, especially while she was watching some interesting program on television, and she would have to scold them in those occasions for them to stop bothering her. But overall they would be loving and respectful of her, "as they should," and even discrete so as to, for instance, allow her for privacy if she wanted to disrobe in order to take a shower or put on her nightgown. I explored whether she would see them or just hear them and she answered, "Doctor, most of the time I can see and hear them as clearly as I can see you, and only sometimes they appear to be a bit fuzzy." She wouldn't need to do anything in particular to evoke their presence. They just simply appeared "on their own will" at her home in the evening, generally after her dinner, sometimes when she least expected them.

Once the theme of those visitations became "normalized" as part of our conversation, I asked her whether, in her view, they were a product of her imagination, ghosts stemming from another dimension, or any other explanation. She said that she wasn't sure: they were probably produced by her imagination, but perhaps not. But she added quickly that she didn't want to dwell on that question because she feared that excessive probing may disturb their visits, which she enjoyed and welcomed, even though they were occasionally tainted with the painful background knowledge that her sons were, of course, dead. And, she added, she had so many struggles and so much suffering in her life that she felt that her current life, including her two loyal daughters and her access to her sons, was like a long-lasting reward "until I join my boys in the afterlife."

I praised her repeatedly for such a creative way of keeping loved people near her, and from then on I didn't probe further on the issue of the materiality of her sons. I should add that, at the end of the first interview, I discontinued all neuroleptics (as their indication was as inappropriate as was her diagnosis at referral[5]) while maintaining, at her request, a prescription of a low dosage of anxiolytics that she would take very occasionally. As predicted, the discontinuation of the neuroleptics resulted in the reduction of her physical discomfort and of her excessive somnolence without any negative consequences.

(continued)

(continued)

The therapeutic encounters continued without major incidents for several months—she would arrive punctually and in a good mood. Our main themes were her relationship with each of her four children, ways of expanding her social network, the support of her health-oriented regime, and a revisitation of episodes of her life. I had the sense that I had become a stable member of her rather meager personal social network and accepted that role without minding it. The lull was interrupted when Samotracia arrived at one of her consultations quite distressed, telling me that her landlord had informed her that they were selling the house where she was renting her small apartment, and that she would have to vacate her dwelling within the following three months. In fact, as a marker of the potentially critical nature of the situation, Samotracia came accompanied by her older daughter (she had joined the consultations a few times before, and had a standing invitation to come with her mother as needed). The daughter, quite concerned, wanted to discuss upfront her concerns with her mother—using me as a catalyst or facilitator, as Samotracia seem to have avoided this theme when the two were alone— and to explore alternatives in what amounted to a severe disturbance in the otherwise calm routines and steady environment of her mother. The daughter proposed to her mother to rent together a larger apartment where daughter, her boyfriend, and mother could live together, while each maintaining their privacy. Samotracia, always careful both not to intrude on her daughter's life and to stake her own independent space, expressed her appreciation but proposed instead that her daughter help her to assess some nearby Spanish-speaking retirement communities that she had heard of through a friend. And so it went: during the following weeks Samotracia and her daughter visited several places until Samotracia, after a couple of false starts, found a satisfactory semi-independent local senior community residency, which the daughter also considered pleasant. There was a short waiting list for a dwelling in that place, and that option became a promising solution. However, during one of the sessions preceding her move, Samotracia confessed to me that one of her main worries was whether her sons would keep on visiting her in the new place, as she would wish. I suggested that it would be a good idea to discuss this specific issue with them during their next visit in her current apartment. (While it had been clear for her that I assumed that her visitors were the product of her imagination, they were regularly included in our conversation with a level of materiality fitting their role as members of her intimate entourage.) She followed my advice and, fortunately, the boys dismissed her concerns, which reduced but did not totally eliminate her distress about the issue. For better or for worse, one of the units became available in that retirement community, and she moved there with the help of her daughters. To her relief, a *few days later she received in her new dwelling the blessed visits of her sons, who teased her gently about characteristics of the new place and about her lack of faith in them until she interrupted that tease in what amounted to a relational routine, namely, she told them they should stop their making fun of her as she wanted to watch her favorite television program. She felt at home again.*

Discussion

As she described it, Samotracia had been raised in an environment of rural poverty, in a small town with scarce access to basic commodities: they lived in adobe houses with dirt floors and no running water or sewage beyond an outhouse and minimal scant access to health or educational resources. At the same time, she had been surrounded by her family as well as a small community that functioned as a family extender. Hence, while suffering the habitual consequences of poverty in developing countries, namely, illiteracy and minimal access to resources, it did not translate itself into an experience of anomy, as is the usual case for the urban very poor and the migrant worker (Sluzki, 1998a, 2010). Most of that changed drastically when she migrated into the United States in search of labor: her personal social network was truncated, and replaced by her boyfriend and later husband, and by occasional work-related relations that would end whenever she or the others shifted jobs and location as one or another harvest was completed. When, years later, she settled in a stable place and with a stable job, she was already the head of household with four children, which forced her to keep two jobs and robbed her of any time to socialize. Samotracia, in spite of her gregarious style, became habituated to a reasonably solitary life. Over time, the loss of her two sons reduced her core family and social world by 50%. However, somehow she managed to retain a thick family connection, both with her daughters, loyally attached to her, and with the almost daily visits of her two sons—a central bond in Latino families (see Falicov, 1998, pp. 170–172). In sum, at present, half of her surrounding family was composed of, so to speak, apparitions. She knew that. However, while at one level she was aware that her visiting sons were of her own creation, at another she did not experience them as puppets whose strings she managed, but as presence with autonomy, agency, and initiative. Her current daily life had all the qualities of the literary style known as *magical realism*—loaded with narratives worthy of a chapter in Gabriel Garcia Marquez's (1991) *One Hundred Years of Solitude*, where reality is supple and the daily life of the characters in the story includes the unusual and the magic.

It should be highlighted that, far from being a characteristic to which Latinos can claim exclusivity, this dual inscription in the "out there" and "in here" world of perceptions and constructions seems to happen quite frequently among people stemming from a variety of non-European cultures, especially those with a sedentary tradition and a low level of literacy, frequently belonging to countries defined by the World Bank as "developing" rather than "developed."[6] This dual inscription can also be explored through the lens of Bakhtin's (1981) "dialogic theory," a worldview where reality is not logically divided into reciprocally exclusive categories, but exists simultaneously in a centrifugal–centripetal (change–sameness, loss–retention) dynamic. This lens is particularly apt to analyze ways in which people out of their original socio-cultural environment negotiate their insertion in the new land, and go through life's gains and losses meshing apparently incompatible worlds and principles in their daily life (DeSantis, 2001).

From that perspective, it merits asking, where is the location of the boundary of Samotracia's (experience of) self? Essentially a construct born within an intra-personal epistemology, a good part of the early literature on the *self* emerged within the psychoanalytic tradition. Taken as point of departure Kohut's (1977) description of the self as the cohesive *experience of being* that regulates the entire person, five clinically significant variables have been described in terms of this experience (Person, Cooper, & Gabbard, 2005): sense of boundaries between self and others; self-esteem or self-worth; sense of wholeness and continuity; genuineness (degree of meshing between the private and the public); and sense of agency. To this could be added what Roland (cited by Falicov, 1998, p. 163), named as the "familial self," a construct that includes close relations as part of who one is.

It merits analyzing Samotracia from this perspective. The value of her sons' presence in her life was clear: they allowed her to retain a sense of wholeness and continuity and provided her with the peace that such a sense brings with it; and, while she maintains a certain level of awareness that these visitors were the product of her imagination—and therefore they "belong" to her—she retains a sense of the skin-bound boundaries of her self through her perception of, and interaction with, her visitors, who are dealt with as *external beings*. In fact, Samotracia's trepidation to move to a new dwelling derived in part from that experience of the autonomy to her apparitions (it is "up to them" to make themselves present), a fear that was congruent with her keeping out of her discourse and of this experience the notion that ultimately she controlled their materialization. In fact, for her to treat the visits of her sons as an obvious product of her imagination would make them less real and risk their vanish altogether. And her relief at their "visit" after her move provided her with the necessary de-coupling of the apparitions from her skin-bound self so as to perceive them as bona fide visitors who were pouring their love to her.

Gergen (1991, especially chapter 7) postulates that, in contemporary, post-modern society, our self constructs and reconstructs itself in its interaction with the myriads of relations in which we are embedded (he refers of the self as a "strategic manipulator of the environment"). But perhaps this is not necessarily only a product of the "saturation of our contemporary life" but a universal trait in the never-ending process of construction and retention of our identity, that becomes more challenged when we become immersed in a society where the retention of a stable, reliable, close social milieu becomes difficult, if not impossible. Further, different cultures prepare us differently to deal with those circumstances, either retrenching the boundaries of the self, or extending it to include the social environment as needed.

My therapeutic endeavor with Samotracia became a strange mixture of: (a) respect and up to a point admiration for her having managed to create a "portable family" that completed her connection with her loved ones and allowed her to receive the modicum of attention, loyalty, and devotion that she needed in order to remain nourished in an otherwise socially impoverished world; (b) neither legitimizing the physicality of her visitors (she would have felt infantilized by that) nor disqualifying their presence (she would have felt alienated from me); (c) involving her *four* offspring in discussions about family issues, including very pragmatic discussions on how to avoid alienating one of Samotracia's daughters while not yielding to that daughter's tendency to overprotect her, as well as how to regulate the "visits of her sons" so as to retain some periods of solitude and privacy that Samotracia also enjoyed. I would occasionally treat those scenarios as "real" with comments along the lines of "You seem to overindulge those boys. What, are you afraid that if you scold them when they annoy you they would cease visiting you?" while being aware that she did not believe that I believed that those embodiments were anything other than the product of her fantasy. However, on other occasions, I would treat her visions as such, asking her, for instance, "Do they appear as having the age they had when you last saw them in life, or are they growing older as times passes?"; (d) revisiting her life and re-historying it in a way that would reconcile her with difficult periods of her past, including suggesting "conversations" with her sons about periods of their life in which she thought she had been a less-than-perfect mother; and (e) facilitating and stimulating the development of new social connections beyond her meager current one, in which the health and mental health services (myself included) played an important role. Of course, in order to legitimize the access to these services it was almost necessary to have the presence of a symptom. To try to avoid that trap, I scheduled her bi-monthly visits as a routine, making it clear that she didn't need to feel anxious or bad or have any symptom whatsoever in order to attend, which she appreciated with an understanding laughter.

In regard to her new dwelling, it ended up becoming an interesting new resource for her, as it was mainly populated by Latino women, including a couple of acquaintances with whom she progressively developed closer friendships.

As therapy evolved, it became evident to me that visiting my office as she did twice a month was one of the highlights of her social life: our understanding of each other within the frame of her history made the conversation easy and, well, familiar. The happy coincidence of her moving to a new dwelling in which sociality was facilitated made more tolerable for her the otherwise complicated reality that, after all that time, I was leaving that area and discontinuing our association. In fact, I referred her to another bilingual colleague to whom I previously discussed this patient, and who agreed wholeheartedly to continue with the tack that I followed.

Having moved geographically a few thousand miles from the region where Samotracia lives, however, I hope that I can visit her occasionally and that I evoke some tender feelings in her, as she has done with me through visiting me in this chapter.

Notes

1 Needless to say, major and prolonged trauma such as years in a concentration camp, months of unending terror in a torture center, the ordeal of captivity for ransom, may lead to major splits in identity, creating fragmented partial selves coexisting in parallel but almost disconnected, unable to fuse or even to have areas in common: one moment I am here, as the socially connected fellow you know, the friend, the parent, the mate, and at the next moment I am back there, in the concentration camp, witnessing myself stealing without remorse bread from a dying inmate, sneaking myself to the back of a formation so that another person will be chosen for the gas chamber, a living dead of sorts (for vivid description of this process, cf. Langer, 1991).

2 How come such an utterly Greek and rather unusual insular name was bestowed at birth on this Mexican-born woman was a mystery not only for me but also for her: she didn't have any satisfactory explanation about what inspired her parents, both semi-analphabet peasants, to give her that name.

3 The Guaraní were the natives of Paraguay and northeast Argentina before the Spanish conquest and are still a substantial part of that region's population. To further reveal some background regarding my empathic connections with this woman, I should add that the nanny who helped raise me during my first years of life and with whom I remained in contact for next sixty years was a sweet Paraguayan woman of Guaraní origin. A reproduction of the engraving mentioned in the text can be found in Moreau/Meffert (1978, p. 242).

4 Latino laborers' personal social network in the United Sates is frequently meager and unstable, weakened by the structure of opportunities that lead them to migrate internally following the pathway of their temporary jobs—for example, harvests—or moving to a major city to enhance their economic status (Menjívar, 2002).

5 A clinical/taxonomic disquisition: once having excluded high fever, confusion, use of hallucinogens, severe sensory impairment such as macular degeneration, delirium and

dementia, and an improbable history of schizophrenia (and visual hallucinations are extremely infrequent in association with that diagnosis), what Samotracia experienced could be labeled, in the classificatory world of Occidental medicine, as *hypnagogic hallucinations*, that is, hallucinations that take place in the twilight process of falling asleep (Slade & Bentall, 1988; Manford & Andermann, 1998; Ohayon, 2000; Ohayon, Priest, Caulet, & Guilleminault, 1996). However, while most hypnagogic hallucinations are experienced as scary, hers were pleasant, expected, and enjoyed. This trait may place Samotracia more in the category of LaBerge's "oneironauts," that is, people capable of self-inducing a state of lucid dreaming (LaBerge & Rheingold, 1997).

In fact, hallucinations spread on a continuum between normal experiences and symptoms of severe psychiatric disturbances. They occur with varying frequency—from once in a lifetime to several times a day—in a 38.7% of the general population (Johns, 2005). Factors positively associated with visual hallucinations include female gender, living alone, older age (Holroyd, Rabins, Finkelstein, & Lavrisha, 1994), diminished visual acuity (Rosenbaum & Freedman, 1987), and meta-cognitive beliefs about hallucinations—that is, assumption that "hallucinations" are normal experiences rather than a sign of psychopathology (Morrison, Wells, & Nothard, 2000; Johns, 2005).

6 See, as another instance, the family described in Chapter 4.

Wrap Up : 8

Let the epilogue begin with a summary. We have visited five families and five diverse therapeutic experiences. In fact, we may add to the list a sixth, more macro-therapeutic experience when one of those interviews was presented and discussed to a larger audience in a very appropriate social moment. We also invited into this book a person who entailed a therapeutic experience for me, while, alas, not vice versa, namely that early patient with a marvelous project to rid the world of nasty people in power while having decimated his own social network, whose fate may have been different had we met several years later, when my ideas were a bit clearer and my omnipotence a bit lessened by the experience of being a practitioner in a specialty that promises more than what it delivers (at least for patients who stubbornly deviated from consensus). To complete this preliminary listing I should add the reference about my favorite cat.

The first family we visited was that tragic victim of tyranny, an amputated family inhabiting a dramatic space of silence and simulation, imprisoned by an environment of threat and ambiguous loss surrounding the virtual presence of a couple of *desaparecidos*. A strong demystifying interview and a most interesting series of follow-up sessions accompanied by a welcomed political decompression provided a view of transformative processes that point to a better future for them all.

That interview was also the vehicle of a collective transformation that, taking place in the right context at the right time, expelled many tyrannical ghosts that were, until that moment, haunting with their oppressive instructions the minds and behaviors of hundreds of colleagues.

The second consultation discussed was the large Moroccan-French family who, as their assigned therapists lamented, behaved "as good patients" during the sessions but didn't find a comfortable balance between cultures both in their daily practices and in their unusual experiences with wolves, dogs, and medusas. Somehow that balance seems to shift when the therapeutic conversation—and the representation between cultures—became more symmetrical and the metaphors less abrasive.

The third one was the trio that reconstituted themselves as a tight four-member family each time they happened to coincide in the same geographic space: the father, who lived in a Caribbean island, the daughter, an itinerant adventurer, the son, marginally anchored in the local community of chronic psychiatric patients, and mother, Madame, floating in the interpersonal ether and perhaps even inhaled by us. Practicalities that seemed to be entangled were clarified and helped, while the collective cult may have remained intact.

The fourth consultation was focused on the young couple with a new daughter and a 4-year-old ghost announcing its presence through his mother's depression, additionally burdened by her husband's apparent emotional disconnection from all that, until his 4-year-old dead brother, visiting him in his dreams, helped him to reconnect with his grief, and with his wife's, lifting her symptoms while transforming them into a shared set of emotions and of actions that may allow them to own the pain—and to let it go at the same time.

And the fifth, good old Samotracia, for whom the material presence of two faithful daughters didn't fill the hole of solitude and pain in her emotional and social life stemming from the loss of her two sons, until their ghostly presence fulfilled her need to have a full (while portable, so to speak) total family, a solution that had been objected and labeled as symptoms by prior custodians of the boundary of what should be considered proper mental health. I may not have done with her much more than undoing prior labeling and accompanying her in a couple of critical life circumstances, but, well, that is not a small feat, considering the alternatives.

Each of these groups inhabited a world that received, on a regular basis, the visits of what we, educated occidentals attached to our pragmatic beliefs, would label as hallucinations or ghosts or apparitions or unusual presences. The first family had a good part of their semantic and behavioral space occupied by a secret—the permanent while unmentionable presence of their *desaparecidos*, maintained in their virtual negative locus by the ominous instructions of the representatives of a repressive public order. The second one was fighting an invasion of dogs, wolves, and other apparitions, as well as that of the norms and mores of their country of adoption, dissonant with, when not contradictory from, those of their own history and traditions. The third family included the persistent virtual existence of Madame, as central in death as she seems to have been while alive, her ghostly rights vehemently defended at least by one of the members of her cult. The fourth one, welcoming the visits of two beloved sons, killed years ago, one in a shootout between south Los Angeles gangs and the other to complications of AIDS. And the fifth family, in which a baby was able to re-enter the world of the mourned by the hand of a four-year-old child, already an inhabitant of that realm. To that we may add many attendants to that professional congress, still entrapped in a world populated by tyrannical instructions not to hear, see, or think forbidden thoughts, so as not to risk terrible consequences.[1]

I hope it has become clear that, throughout these interviews and interventions, and in the subsequent discussion of these processes, my primary interest was neither to elicit ghosts nor to explore possible (and generally oversimplified and elusive) causes or origins of the problems or issues that may have brought them to the consultation. At the same time, the cultural clashes that reverberated in the Moroccan family and in Samotracia prior story, and the repressive political context in both the consultation and my presentation of the family with *desaparecidos*' became crucial contextual referents.

My first impression—my first reflections immediately after those interviews or therapies took place—has been that I attempted to destabilize traits of the collective story as provided by the family. In all I utilized both my and their resources as well as therapeutic instruments within what could be called the narrative spectrum, such as circular questions, positive connotations, reframing, externalization, and naiveté (i.e., avoiding adopting premises implied in, or underlying, their assertions), while maintaining a respectful style of contact. At the broadest level, I seem to operate with what Helm Stierlin labeled "systemic optimism" (Stierlin, 1988), namely, the educated assumption that our therapeutic participation following systemic premises will help the family to evolve in a favorable direction, regardless of the specific symptom or problem that triggered the consultation.[2]

Throughout these chapters I propose here and there possible causal hypotheses about what lead a family to generate, adopt or maintain a given symptomatic or problematic narrative. I should clarify that, rather than strong guiding beliefs, those have been in most cases *a posteriori* constructs, suggested so as to generate an elegant bow that may provide closure to the stories displayed during the interview. However, and as a cautionary note, simple causal explanations risk oversimplifying the inherent complexity of the intrinsically chaotic, multi-determined nature of the process of change in human systems.

There are many therapists, however, who operate with the conviction that there are themes that contain the key to unveil the roots of most conflict. Such is the case of colleagues who assume that the core key toward the elucidation of conflicts and emotional distress lies in disturbances in the intergenerational chain—secret alliances, obfuscations, mandates, and injunctions. Others will focus on incomplete mourning and unresolved losses, and still others on cross-cultural clashes experienced by the current and/or previous generations, or on cultural clashes, present or remote in the family history, or in complications in the autonomy–dependency dialectic. And, with admirable frequency, consultations with therapists yield their favorite themes as Gordian knots, their resolution involving family and therapists with interest and intensity, rewarding them with many therapeutic successes. As I see it ("and therefore I believe it," as would Heinz von Foerster, in order to challenge the direction of the process of reality construction), these therapists, and perhaps all therapists are, to a greater or lesser degree, specialists in listening and talking about their favorite subjects. But it happens that those broad subjects—family of origin, loss and mourning, cultural traditions and clashes, dependency and autonomy, and a few others—are universal "strange attractors," themes with which people resonate almost universally, and around which we can weave meaningful, emotionally loaded, stories (Sluzki, 1998b). However, it is the focal exploration and selective listening of those therapists, who are reasonably guided by their conceptual premises, that establishes the thematic focus of those therapeutic encounters, and not necessarily the emergence of a root problem attributed to the family's (or the individual's) reason for consultation. Needless to say, if those therapists become well known in terms of their favored thematic skills, they will, with time, be sought for therapy by individuals, couples, or families for whom those themes resonate, creating an elegant process of confirmation of the conceptual premises of both therapist and patients.

This should not be construed as a criticism to therapists with thematic preferences. After all, in the vast majority of cases those preferences are reasonably guided in good faith and professional responsibility by the therapists' own dominant conceptual assumptions. We may agree or disagree with their thematic or conceptual centrality, but, if we vehemently question that dominance, it is in all likelihood because we are faithful with equal vehemence to our own models and their attached thematic orientation. Each one of us has, indeed, favorite themes and thematic blind zones, and is biased in favor of the former while ignoring the latter. To rephrase this argument with words currently en vogue, we all co-construct the narratives that nest problems and their possible (dis)solution with our patients, and the "co-" is in tune with our conceptual and personal resonances (Elkaim, 1997; Cyrulnik & Elkaim, 2009).[3]

In this regard I should underscore that the presence of ghosts, or the suspicion about their possible presence, is *not* a part of my own prior assumptions or conceptual premises about the scenarios where conflicts are nested, nor, as far as I know, do individuals, couples, or families who have consulted me have assumptions about ghosts or any special skills of mine to conjure and exorcise them. In fact, I found each of the consultations discussed in this book moving as well as fascinating to work with and, later, to revisit as I was becoming interested in "fantastic realism" as an esthetic current and, in at least one of them, because of my active involvement in human rights. These clinical experiences are among many that have filled my years of practice and, only after the fact, over the years, came together on their own. I found these narratives not only attractive, but also a relevant vehicle for allowing some rumination about culture and the boundaries of the self that accompanied them as commentaries throughout this volume.

Notes

1 I had other opportunities to work on this specific subject with professionals from countries that were emerging from political dictatorships, with similar liberating effects (cf. Sluzki, 1994).

2 I should rush to add a second layer of assumptions that orients my work, along the lines of social constructionism and its tie-in, the narrative approach—strongly influenced by my frequent association at different moments with Paul Watzlawick, Heinz von Foerster, Michael White, Gianfranco Cecchin, Marcelo Pakman, and, indeed, Sara Cobb.

3 This benign, slightly ecumenical stance doesn't extend to practices that foster dependency on the therapist, plant memories, or favor indoctrination of any kind.

References

Abudabbeh, N. (2005). Arab families: an overview. In M. McGoldrick, J. Gordano, & J. K. Pearce (eds.), *Ethnicity and Family Therapy*, 3rd. edition. New York: Guilford, pp. 423–436.

Alexy, T. (1993). *The Mezuzah in the Madonna's Foot: Marranos and Other Secret Jews—A Woman Discovers her Spiritual Heritage*. New York: Simon & Schuster.

Amnesty International (1975). *Report on Torture*. New York: Farrar, Straus & Giroux.

Amnesty International (1987). *Report*. London: Amnesty International.

Andersen, T. (1991). *The Reflecting Team: Dialogues and Dialogues about Dialogues*. New York: W.W. Norton.

Arendt, H. (1958). *The Human Condition*. Chicago: University of Chicago Press.

Armon-Jones, C. (1986). The social functions of emotion. In R. Harre (ed.), *The Social Construction of Emotions*. Oxford and New York: Basil Blackwell.

Avruch, K. (2003). Type I and type II errors in culturally sensitive conflict resolution practice. *Conflict Resolution Quarterly*, 20(3): 351–371.

Bakhtin, M. (1981). *The Dialogic Imagination: Four Essays*. Austin: University of Texas Press.

Bateson, G. (1972). *Steps to an Ecology of Mind*. New York: Ballantine.

Bateson, G., Jackson, D.D., Haley, J., & Weakland, J.H. (1956). Toward a theory of schizophrenia. *Behavioral Science*, 1(4): 251–264.

Boss, P.G. (1984). The relationship of psychological father presence, wife's personal qualities, and wife/family dysfunction in families of missing fathers. *Journal of Marriage and the Family*, 42: 541–549.

Boss, P.G. (1988). *Family Stress Management*. Newbury Park CA: Sage.

Boss, P.G. (2006). *Loss Trauma and Resilience: Therapeutic Work with Ambiguous Loss*. New York: W.W. Norton.

Boss, P.G., & Greenberg, J. (1984). Family boundary ambiguity new variable in family stress theory. *Family Process*, 23: 535–546.

Buckley, W. (1967). *Sociology and Modern Systems Theory*. Englewood Cliffs, NJ: Prentice Hall.

Camarasa, J., Felice, R., & Gonzalez, D. (1985). *El juicio: Proceso al horror*. Buenos Aires: Sudamericana/Planeta.

Castaneda, C. (1968). *The Teachings of Don Juan: A Yaqui Way of Knowledge*. New York: Washington Square Press.

Catoggio, M.S. (2010). The last military dictatorship in Argentina (1976–1983): The mechanism of state terrorism. *Online Encyclopedia of Mass Violence*, published on 5 July, 2010, accessed October 7, 2012. URL: www.massviolence.org/The-Last-Military-Dictatorship-in-Argentina-1976-1983-the?decoupe_recherche=%20Catoggio (accessed October 7, 2012).

Cecchin, G. (1987). Hypothesizing, circularity and neutrality revisited: An invitation to curiosity. *Family Process*, 26(4): 405–413.

Cecchin G., Lane, G., & Ray, W.A. (1994). *The Cybernetics of Prejudice in the Practice of Psychotherapy*. London: Karnac.

Center for Immigration Studies (2012). www.cis.org/2012-profile-of-americas-foreign-born-population (accessed August 8, 2013).

Cobb, S. (2013). *Speaking of Violence: The Politics and Poetics of Narrative in Conflict Resolution*. Oxford and New York: Oxford University Press.

Cobb, S. (2013b). Narrative "braiding" and the role of public officials in transforming the public's conflict. *Narrative and Conflict: Explorations of Theory and Practice,* 1(1): 4–30.

CONADEP (1984). *Nunca Mas: Informe de la Comision Nacional sobre la desaparicion de personas*. Buenos Aires: EUDEBA. (English edition: *Never Again: Argentina's National Commission on Disappeared People*. 1986. London and Boston: Faber & Faber in association with Index on Censorship.) Also available at www.nuncamas.org.

Corradi, J.E. (1985). *The Fitful Republic: Economy, Society, and Politics in ARGENTINA*. Boulder, CO: Westview Press.

Corradi, J.E., Weiss Fagen, P., & Garreton, M.A. (1992). *Fear at the Edge: State Terror and Resistance in Latin America*. Berkeley: University of California Press.

Correia Da Cunha, A. (1982). *Dicionario Etimologico Nova Fronteira da Lingua Portuguesa*. Rio de Janeiro: Editora Nova Fronteira.

Cortazar, J. (1985). *Blow-Up and Other Stories* (originally published as *End of the Game and Other Stories*). New York: Pantheon.

Cyrulnik, B., & Elkaim, M. (2009). *Entre resilience et resonance*. Ed. C. Maestre. Paris: Fabert.

DeSantis, A.D. (2001). Caught between two worlds: Bakhtin's dialogism in the exile experience. *Journal of Refugee Studies,* 14(1): 1–10.

De Shazer, S. (1985). *Keys to Solutions in Brief Therapy*. New York: W.W. Norton.

Droeven, J., & Crescini, S. (1987). Effectos de la violencia represive: Familias con miembros desaparecidos (Effects of the repressive violence: Families with disappeared members). *Sistemas Familiares*, 3(2): 7–15.

Dyche, L., & Zayas, L.H. (1995). The value of curiosity and naiveté for the cross-cultural psychotherapist. *Family Process*, 34(4): 389–399.

Elkaim, M. (1997). *If You Love Me, Don't Love Me: Undoing Reciprocal Double Binds and Other Methods of Change in Couple and Family Therapy*. New York: Jason Aronson.

Falicov, C. (ed.) (1986). *Cultural Perspectives in Family Therapy*. Rockville, MD: Aspen.

Falicov, C. (1995). Training to think culturally: A multidimensional comparative framework. *Family Process*, 34(4): 373–388.

Falicov, C.J. (1998). *Latino Families in Therapy: A Guide to Multicultural Practice*. New York: Guilford Press.

Falk, J. (1980). The conversational duet. *Proceedings of the Sixth Annual Meeting of the Berkeley Linguistic Society*, 507–514.

Fisch, R., Weakland, J.H., & Segal, L. (1982). *The tactics of Change: Doing Therapy Briefly*. San Francisco: Jossey-Bass.

Furman, B., & Ahola, T. (1992). *Solution Talk: Hosting Therapeutic Conversations*. New York: W.W. Norton.

Garcia Marquez, G. (1967/1991). *One Hundred Years of Solitude*. New York: Harper-Collins.

Gergen, K.J. (1991). *The Saturated Self: Dilemmas of Identity in Contemporary Life*. New York: Basic Books.

Goldhagen, D.J. (1996). *Hitler's Willing Executioners: Ordinary Germans and the Holocaust*. New York: Knopf.

Graziano, F. (1992). *Divine Violence: Spectacle, Psychosexuality & Radical Christianity in the Argentine "Dirty War"*, Boulder, San Francisco, and Oxford: Westview.

Holroyd, S., Rabins, P.V., Finkelstein, D., & Lavrisha, M. (1994). Visual hallucinations in patients from an ophthalmology clinic and medical clinic population. *J Nerv Ment Dis,* 182: 273–276.

Horowitz, M. (1985). Disasters and psychological responses to stress. *Psychiatric Annals,* 15(3): 161–167.

Hunter, E.J. (1983). Treating the military captive family. In F. Kaslow & R. Ridenour (eds.), *The Military Family: Dynamics and Treatment*. New York: Guilford Press.

International Office for Migration (2013). *World Migration Report 2013: Migrant Well Being and Development*. Geneva, Switzerland: IOM.

Johns, L.C. (2005). Hallucinations in. *Current Psychiatric Reports* 7(3): 162–167.

Kohen, C. (1988). Political traumas, oppression, and rituals. In E.E. Black, J. Roberts, & R. Whiting (eds.), *Rituals in Families and Family Therapy*. New York: W.W. Norton.

Kohut, H. (1977). *The Restoration of the Self*. New York: International Universities Press.

LaBerge, S., & Rheingold, S. (1997). *Exploring the World of Lucid Dreaming*. New York: Ballantine Books.

Laing, R.D., Phillipson, H., & Lee, A.R. (1972). *Interpersonal Perception: A Theory and a Method of Research*. New York: Perennial.

Langer, L.L. (1991). *Holocaust Testimonies: The Ruins of Memory*. New Haven: Yale University Press.

Laub, D. (1992). Bearing witness or the vicissitudes of listening. In S. Feldman and D. Laub (eds.), *Testimony: Crisis of Witnessing in Literature, Psychoanalysis and History*. New York and London: Routledge.

Laub, D., & Auerhahn, N.C. (1993). Knowing and not knowing—massive psychic trauma: Forms of traumatic memory. *International Journal of Psycho-Analysis,* 74: 287–302.

Manford, M., & Andermann, F. (1998). Complex visual hallucinations. Clinical and Neurobiological insights. *Brain,* 121(10): 1819–1840.

Marchak, P. (1999). *God's Assassins: State Terrorism in Argentina in the 1970s*. Quebec: McGill-Queens University Press.

McFarlane, W.R., Dixon, L., Lukens, E., & Lucksted, A. (2007). Family psychoeducation and schizophrenia: A review of the literature. *Journal of Marital and Family Therapy,* 29(2): 223–245.

McGoldrick, M. (ed.) (1998). *Re-Visioning Family Therapy: Race, Culture and Gender in Clinical Practice*. New York: Guilford Press (2nd edition, 2007).

McGoldrick, M., & Walsh, F. (2004). *Living Beyond Loss; Death in the Family*, 2nd edition. New York: W.W. Norton.

McGoldrick, M., Giordano, J., & Pearce, J.K. (eds.) (2005). *Ethnicity and Family Therapy*, 3rd edition. New York: Guilford.

Menjivar, C. (2002). *Fragmented Ties: Salvadoran Immigrant Networks in America*. Berkeley: University of California Press.

Migration News (2003). Volume 10, number 1. University of California Davis.

Minuchin, S. (1974). *Families & Family Therapy*. Cambridge, MA: Harvard University Press.

Minuchin, S. (1987). My many voices. In J.K. Zeig (ed.), *The Evolution of Psychotherapy*. New York: Brunner/Mazel, pp. 5–14.

Mollica, R.F. (1988). The trauma story: Psychiatric care of refugee survivors. In F.M. Ochberg (ed.), *Post-traumatic Therapy and Victims of Violence*. New York: Brunner/Mazel.

Moreau, C., & Meffert, C. (1978). *Clément Moreau/Carl Meffert: Grafik für den Mitmenschen.* Berlin: Neue Gesellschaft für bildende Kunst.

Morrison, A.P., Wells, A., & Nothard, S. (2000). Cognitive factors in predisposition to auditory and visual hallucinations. *British Journal of Clinical Psychology*, 39: 67–78.

Muñoz, L., Marconi, J., Horwitz, J., & Naveillan, P. (1966). Cross-cultural definitions applied to the study of functional Psychoses in Chilean Mapuches. *Brit J Psychiatry*, 112: 1205–1215.

Ohayon, M.M. (2000). Prevalence of hallucinations and their pathological association in the general population. *Psychiatric Research*, 97: 153–164.

Ohayon, M.M,. Priest, R.E.G., Caulet, M., & Guilleminault, C. (1996). Hyponagogic and hypnopompic hallucinations: Pathological phenomena? *British Journal of Psychiatry*, 169: 459–467.

Paul, N. (1986). The Paradoxical nature of the grief experience. *Contemporary Family Therapy*, 8(1): 5–19.

Paul, N. & Grosser, G.H. (1965). Operational mourning and its role in conjoint family therapy. *Community Mental Health Journal*, 1(4): 336–346.

Person, E.S., Cooper, A.M., & Gabbard, G.O. (2005). *Textbook of Psychoanalysis.* Washington, DC: American Psychiatric Press.

Pichon-Riviere, E. (2001). *El Proceso Grupal (Del psicoanálisis a la psicología Social, I).* Buenos Aires: Ediciones Nueva Visión.

Ritterman, M. (1985). Symptoms, social justice and personal freedom. *Journal of Strategic and Systemic Therapies*, 4(2): 48–63.

Rose, S.L., & Garske, J. (1987). Family environment, adjustment and coping among children of holocaust survivors. *American Journal of Orthopsychiatry*, 57: 332–344.

Rosenbaum, F., & Freedman, M. (1987). Visual hallucinations in sane people: Charles Bonnet syndrome. *Journal of Geriatric Psychiatry and Neurology*, 35: 66–68.

Rosenhan, D.L. (1973). On being sane in insane places. *Science*, 179(1): 250–258.

Scarry, E. (1985). *The Body in Pain: The Making and Unmaking of the World.* New York: Oxford University Press.

Selvini Palazzoli, M., Boscolo, L., Cecchin, G., & Prata, G. (1980). Hypothesizing-circularity-neutrality: Three guidelines for the conduction of the session. *Family Process*, 19(1): 3–12.

Selvini Palazzoli, M., Cirillo, S., Selvini, M., & Sorrentino, A. (1989). *Family Games: General Model of Psychotic Processes in the Family.* New York: W.W. Norton.

Singer, M.T., & Lalich, J. (1996). *Cults in our Midst: The Hidden Menace if our Everyday Lives.* San Francisco, Jossey Bass.

Slade, P.D., & Bentall, R.P. (1988). *Sensory Deception: A Scientific Analysis of Hallucination.* Baltimore, MD: Johns Hopkins University Press.

Sluzki, C.E. (1961). Trifluorperazine in the treatment of chronic delusions. *Acta Neuropsiquiat. Arg.*, 7: 136–140.

Sluzki, C.E. (1979). Migration and family conflict. *Family Process*, 18(4): 379–390.

Sluzki, C.E. (1983). Bumping against walls: Resistance as a misnomer. Audio-cassette. In Aponte H., Sluzki, C.E., Anderson, C., Papp. P., Wachtel, P., &. Wachtel, E., *From Resistance to Alliance in Family Therapy: New Perspectives and Techniques.* New York: BMA Audio Cassette Publications.

Sluzki, C.E. (1992a). Network disruption and network reconstruction in the process of migration/relocation. *Family Systems Medicine*, 10(4): 359–364.

Sluzki, C.E. (1992b). The "better-formed" story. In G. Cecchin and M. Mariotti (eds.), *L'Adolescente e i suoi Sistemi.* Rome: Kappa, pp. 37–47 (in Italian).

Sluzki, C.E. (1993). Toward a general model of family and political victimization. *Psychiatry*, 56: 178–187. Also as a chapter in D.F. Schnitman (ed.), *New Paradigms, Culture and Subjectivity*. New York: Hampton Press.

Sluzki, C.E. (1994). Reclaiming words, reclaiming worlds. *Readings: A Journal of Reviews and Commentary in Mental Health*, 9(2): 4–7.

Sluzki, C.E. (1997). *The Social Network, Frontier of Systemic Practices*. Buenos Aires: Gedisa (in Spanish; also in Portuguese: Rio de Janeiro, Casa do Psicologo, 1998).

Sluzki, C.E. (1998a). Migration and the disruption of the social network. In McGoldrick, M. (ed.), *Re-Visioning Family Therapy: Race, Culture and Gender in Clinical Practice*. New York: Guilford Press (2nd edition, 2007).

Sluzki, C.E. (1998b). Strange attractors and the transformation of narratives in therapy. In Hoyt, M.F. (ed.), *The Handbook of Constructive Therapies*. San Francisco: Jossey Bass.

Sluzki, C.E. (2000). Patients, clients, consumers: The politics of words. *Family, Systems and Health*, 18(3): 347–352.

Sluzki, C.E. (2010). Personal social networks and health: Conceptual and clinical implications of their reciprocal impact. *Family Systems and Health*, 28(1): 1–18.

Stierlin, H. (1988). Systemic optimism—systemic pessimism: Two perspectives on change. *Family Process*, 27(2): 123–127.

Tomm, K. (1987). Interventive interviewing: Part II. Reflexive questioning as a means to enable self-healing. *Family Process*, 26(2): 167–183.

Tomm, K. (1988). Interventive interviewing: Part III, Intending to ask lineal, circular, strategic, reflexive questions? *Family Process*, 27(1): 1–15.

Tomm, K. (1989). Externalizing the problem and internalizing personal agency. *Journal of Strategic and Systemic Therapies*, 8: 16–22.

Verbitsky, H. (1996). *The Flight. Confessions of an Argentine Dirty Warrior*. New York: New Press.

Waschler, L. (1990). *A Miracle, A Universe: Settling Accounts with Torturers*. New York: Pen.

Weber-Rouget, B., & Jean-Michel Aubry, J.-M. (2007). Efficacy of psychoeducational approaches on bipolar disorders: A review of the literature. *Journal of Affective Disorders*, 98(1–2): 11–27.

White, M. (1984). Pseudo-encopresis: From avalanche to victory, from vicious to virtuous circles. *Family Systems Medicine* 2(2): 150–160.

White, M., & Epston, D. (1990). *Narrative Means to Therapeutic Ends*. New York: W.W. Norton.

Names Index

Abudabbeh, N. 66n5
Ahola, T. 87
Alexy, T. 66n2
Andermann, F. 99n5
Andersen, T. 82, 88n2
Arendt, H. 41
Armon-Jones, C. 44n6
Aubry, J.-M. 88n3
Auerhahn, N.C. 42
Avruch, K. 45

Bakhtin, M. 96
Bateson, G. 32n2, 77
Bentall, R.P. 99n5
Boscolo, L. 81
Boss, P.G. 11, 29, 30
Brea, M. 44n8
Buckley, W. 33n9

Camarasa, J. 13
Castaneda, C. 3
Catoggio, M.S. 13
Caulet, M. 99n5
Cecchin, G. 7, 46, 78, 81, 104n2
Cirillo, S. 78
Cobb, S. 80, 104n2
Cooper, A.M. 96
Corradi, J.E. 12, 13
Correia da Cunha, A. 89
Cortazar, J. 66n1

Crescini, S. 29, 30, 31
Cyrulnik, B. 103

De Shazer, S. 87
DeSantis, A.D. 96
Dixon, L. 88n3
Droeven, J. 29, 30, 31
Dyche, L. 46

Elkaim, M. 70, 103
Epston, D. 81, 87

Falicov, C.J. 45, 46, 47, 95, 96
Falk, J. 82
Felice, R. 13
Finkelstein, D. 99n5
Fisch, R. 87
Freedman, M. 99n5
Furman, B. 87

Gabbard, G.O. 96
Garcia Marquez, G. 3, 95
Garreton, M.A. 13
Garske, J. 31
Gergen, K.J. 97
Giordano, J. 45
Giordano de Guilligan, J. 33n7
Goldhagen, D.J. 43n1
Gonzalez, D. 13
Goodall, J. 72

Graziano, F. 12
Greenberg, J. 30
Grosser, G.H. 86
Guilleminault, C. 99n5

Haley, J. 32n2
Hoffman, D. 72
Holroyd, S. 99n5
Hopkins, A. 72
Horowitz, M. 30
Horwitz, J. 9n5
Hunter, E.J. 30

Jackson, D.D. 32n2
Johns, L.C. 99n5

Kahlbaum, K. 79n1
Kohen, C. 29, 30
Kohut, H. 96
Kraepelin, E. 79n1

LaBerge, S. 99n5
Laing, R.D. 2
Lane, G. 78
Langer, L.L. 40, 98n1
Laub, D. 42, 44n9
Lavrisha, M. 99n5
Lee, A.R. 2
Lévi-Strauss, C. 62
Lucksted, A. 88n3
Lukens, E. 88n3

Manford, M. 99n5
Marchak, P. 13
Marconi, J. 9n5
McFarlane, W.R. 88n3
McGoldrick, M. 45, 86
Meffert, C. 98n3
Menjivar, C. 98n4
Minuchin, S. 4, 31,
   79n2
Mollica, R.F. 29
Moreau, C. 91, 98n3
Morrison, A.P. 99n5
Muñoz, L. 9n5

Naveillan, P. 9n5
Nothard, S. 99n5

Ohayon, M.M. 99n5

Pakman, M. 104n2
Paul, N. 4, 43n4, 86
Pearce, J.K. 45
Peron, J. 11
Person, E.S. 96
Phillipson, H. 2
Pichon-Riviere, E. 2
Prata, G. 81
Priest, R.E.G. 99n5

Rabins, P.V. 99n5
Ray, W.A. 78
Rheingold, S. 99n5
Ritterman, M. 29
Roland, - 96
Rose, S.L. 31
Rosenbaum, F. 99n5
Rosenhan, D.L. 9n5

Santayana, G. 38
Scarry, E. 11, 29, 31
Segal, L. 87
Selvini, M. 78, 81
Selvini Palazzoli, M. 78
Slade, P.D. 99n5
Sluzki, C.E. 9n4, 29, 31, 44n5, 47, 66n6,
   68, 77, 86, 88n1, 95, 103, 104n1
Sorrentino, A. 78
Stalin, J. 44n7
Stierlin, H. 102

Tomm, K. 81, 87

Verbitsky, H. 13
Von Foerster, H. 103, 104n2

Walsh, F. 86
Waschler, L. 41
Watzlawick, P. 104n2
Weakland, J.H. 32n2, 87
Weber-Rouget, B. 88n3
Weiss Fagen, P. 13
Wells, A. 99n5
White, M. 81, 87, 104n2

Zayas, L.H. 46

Subject Index

abandonment, fear of 26
abductions 12–13, 35–36, 44n8; *see also*
   desaparecidos; the "disappeared"
acculturation 64, 65–66
agency 95, 96
Alzheimer's disease 29–30
ambiguous loss 8, 11, 29–30
Amnesty International 13, 29, 36
anchoring 5, 87
"Ancient Cult of Madame" 74–78
animals 2, 26
anomy 95
anti-intellectualism 35
anti-Semitism 35
aporia 11
Arab families 67n5
Argentina 6, 10–33, 34–39, 40, 44n8
Argentinian therapists 6, 14, 15, 25,
   34–39, 41–13
Auschwitz-Birgenau 11, 39–40, 43n4
autonomy 31, 76, 95, 96, 102–103
ayahuasca 3

"being there" 70
beliefs 47–48, 69, 92, 99n5, 101
bereavement 83–86, 92, 95;
  see also loss
"better-formed stories" 5, 87
boundaries of the self 96, 97, 104
braiding 80

Brazil 3
burials, symbolic 75–76, 78

Cambodia 44n7
Candomblé cult 3
Catholic Church 13
children: Argentinian family 14–28;
   kidnapped or disappeared 29, 30,
   33n5; Moroccan immigrant family
   50–66; talking about children in the
   third person 18; torture of 33n5
Chile 9n5, 11, 81
Chinese Cultural Revolution 44n7
circular questions 56, 59, 81, 102
client/patient terminology 9n4
collective witnessing 41
CONADEP 13, 28, 33n5, 39
conceptual models 70
constructionism 70, 104n2
constructivism 86
context 87
continuity 96
"conversational duet" 82
couple therapy 81–86, 88
cultural adaptation 7, 64
cultural boundaries 48, 64
cultural clash 90, 102, 103
cultural identity 47
cultural ignorance 45, 46
cultural practices 31

cultural sensitivity 45, 65
cultural specificity 45–46
cultural transition 47
"culture of fear" 13
curiosity 7, 46, 78, 81

death 13, 20, 40, 42, 73, 84; *see also*
  bereavement
de-labeling 7, 56
delirium tremens 3, 8n4
delusions 69
depression 7, 14, 81, 82, 84, 86, 101
desaparecidos 6, 11, 12, 15, 36, 39,
  40, 100, 101, 102; *see also* the
  "disappeared"
developing countries 95, 96
dialogic theory 96
dictatorships 11, 35–36, 43, 44n6,
  104n1; *see also* State repression
"dirty war" 11–12, 40
the "disappeared" 10, 11, 12, 32n3, 33n5,
  42; family interview 16, 18–19, 27–28,
  29, 30; therapists' work with 35, 39;
  see also desaparecidos
disaster survivors 31
discharge after hospitalization 69
dominant narratives 77
dormitive principles 77
"double-bind" 11, 32n2
dreams 7, 56–60, 62, 63, 84, 85, 99n5;
  see also nightmares
drug use 3

elderly people 7–8
emotions 42, 44n6, 87; bottled-up 86;
  negative 88n3; shared 101; symptoms
  correlated with 23, 24, 32; therapists
  25, 37, 38, 43, 70, 75
empathy 78, 91
enmeshment 22, 31
ethnicity 46
executions 13
exorcism 7, 41, 74–75
expectations 5, 71, 72, 77, 88n3
external world 2
externalization 81, 87, 102

familial self 96
family ecology 31

family evolutionary cycle 46, 48
family interviews *see* interviews
family order 59, 60, 62, 67n5
family stories *see* stories
family therapy 36, 45, 47, 65, 71
fantasies 52
fear 13, 38
France 47, 48, 65
"freezing" of time 30
furor sanandi 7

gender roles 48, 55, 63, 64
genuineness 96
ghost limbs 2, 8n2
ghosts 3–4, 7, 52, 66, 80–81, 101–102,
  103; "Ancient Cult of Madame"
  74–75; Argentinian family 23, 24,
  100; definition of 8n3; exorcising
  41; stillborn child 86, 101; *see also*
  hallucinations
goals of therapy 69–70, 71, 72, 75, 77
grief 12, 31, 38, 44n4, 101
group therapy 35, 36
Guarani 98n3
guiding models 70, 77
guilt 29, 39, 90

hallucinations 3, 89; factors associated
  with 99n5; hypnagogic 99n5; Mapuche
  Indians 9n5; Moroccan immigrant
  family 7, 49, 51, 52–56, 65; visitations
  from dead sons 92–93, 94–95, 96, 97,
  101
health problems 22–23, 84, 91
high boundary ambiguity 29
Holocaust 11, 31, 39–40, 43n4
"honorary parents" 21–22, 25
hopelessness 41, 49
hypnagogic hallucinations 99n5

identity 76, 97, 98n1; *see also* self
the "imaginary" 4
immigrants 6–7, 47–66, 67n3, 91–92
incest 53, 67n5
intake process 5
internal world 2
internalized oppressive instructions 29,
  36
International Criminal Court 32n1

interviews 4–5; Argentinian family
14–30, 37, 41–43; couple therapy
81–86; interviewing "technology" 81;
Moroccan immigrant family 47–66
intra-familial conflicts 47, 48–49, 65, 71,
72
Israel 65

Jews 35, 40, 43n1, 63
joining process 5
joy 90

Khmer Rouge 11, 44n7
"knowing and not knowing" 30, 42

Latinos 31, 90, 95, 96, 98
letting go 2, 8, 101
loss 89–90, 103; ambiguous 8, 11,
29–30; of stillborn child 83–86;
traumatic 86
LSD 3

"Madame, Ancient Cult of"
74–78
Madres de Plaza de Mayo 12, 32n3, 36,
39
"magical", concept of 51, 52, 55
magical (fantastic) realism 7–8, 24, 95,
104
Mapuche Indians 9n5
marijuana 3
materialization 7, 74, 81, 96
medication 68–69, 82, 90, 91,
93
memorabilia 74
memories 39; "ruins of memory" 40;
traumatic memory 42
metaphors 24, 62, 101
Mexico 3, 90, 91
migration 46–47, 98n4
"moments of insight" 80
Moroccan immigrant family 6–7, 47–66,
101
morphogenesis 31, 33n9
morphostasis 31, 33n9
mother, absent 72–78
mourning 42, 86, 103
multidimensionality 46
"multiple voices" 4, 79n2

Muslim identity 48, 49, 54, 63, 67n4,
67n5
mystification 10, 11, 29, 32n2

naiveté 46, 81, 102
narratives 5–6; co-construction of 103;
destabilization of 48, 78, 87, 88n1,
102; dominant 77; esthetic principle
85; problem-based 80, 81, 87;
symptom-based 86; *see also* stories
National Commission on the
Disappearance of Individuals
(CONADEP) 13, 28, 33n5, 39
Nazi regime 12, 32n4, 35
"Night and fog" 12, 32n4
nightmares 3, 7, 40, 52–53, 56–60, 65,
66, 84
normalization 27, 93
norms 47, 64, 65–66
nostalgic longing 89

One Hundred Years of Solitude 3, 95
"oneironauts" 99n5
one-way mirrors 14, 15, 16, 25, 71, 75,
81, 85
oppression 8, 29, 33n8

paraphrenia 68, 79n1
particularism 46
pathology 8
patients 9n4
patriarchy 55, 67n5, 67n7
pavor nocturnus 65
peyote 3
poetry 76, 77
political climate 6, 11–14, 16, 30
positive connotations 81, 102
post-partum depression 7, 81, 82, 84,
86, 101
poverty 95
"powerful attractors" 16, 86
problem-saturated stories 80–81, 87
professional self 70
psychiatric care 68–69, 72, 73, 74, 90
psychiatric symptoms 52, 90, 99n5,
101
psychoanalysis 34–36
psychoeducational approaches 88n3
psychosis 79n1

psychosomatics 22, 31
"psychotic games" 78

the "real" 4
reality 36, 40–41, 42, 47, 48, 70,
    96
"reflective teams" 82, 88n2
reformulations 5
reframing 102
relationships 87
reparative practice 42
repression, State 10–14, 29, 30–31, 35,
    38, 40, 44n5
resistance 77
resonances 70, 103
rituals 4, 21, 44n4, 57, 78, 81, 86, 87
"ruins of memory" 40
Rwandan genocide 11

saudades 89–90
schizophrenia 4, 7, 71, 73, 75, 87,
    99n5
second-hand victimization 39
secrecy 10, 29, 39
self 2–3, 87; boundaries of the 96, 97,
    104; construction and reconstruction
    of the 97; definition of the 2;
    fragmentation of the 98n1; functional
    split of the 90; professional 70
self-blame 85
self-esteem 96
semantic style 18
senses 2, 4
shame 38–39, 42
silence 10, 12–13, 20, 29, 44n4; codes of
    18, 42; victims 40
social constructionism 70, 104n2
social isolation 26, 31, 64, 78, 95
social networks 7, 78, 92, 94, 95, 100;
    Argentinian family 29, 31; Latino
    laborers 98n4; Moroccan immigrant
    family 64
social support 31, 69
Soviet Union 44n7
Spain 35
spiral of reciprocal perspectives 2
State repression 10–13, 29, 30–31, 35,
    38, 40, 44n5
stillborn child 83–86, 101

stories 70, 78; "better-formed" 5, 87;
    problem-saturated 80–81, 87, 88n1;
    transformed 87; universal themes 103;
    see also narratives
"strange attractors" 103
stress 22, 23
structural equation, Lévi-Straussian
    62
suffering 48
suicide 69
suppression of the witness 39–41
"survivor's guilt" 39
systemic optimism 102

"tangible presence" 2
therapeutic interviews 4–5; Argentinian
    family 14–30, 37, 41–43; couple
    therapy 81–86; interviewing
    "technology" 81; Moroccan immigrant
    family 47–66
therapeutic relationship 5, 70
therapists: Argentinian 6, 14, 15, 25,
    34–39, 41–43; cultural sensitivity 45;
    cultural specificity 45–46; elucidation
    of conflicts 102–103; guiding models
    70, 77; mesmerization of 7; Moroccan
    immigrant family 49–50, 56, 63,
    65, 66; thematic focus of 79n4, 103;
    therapist's style 5, 70; witnessing by
    48, 85; working with different cultures
    47–48
"thought reform" 41
time 29, 30, 89–90
titles of therapeutic sessions 69
torture 11, 12, 13, 29, 31, 40, 42; of
    children 33n5; Nazi regime 32n4;
    therapists 35, 36
totalitarianism 39, 44n7; see also
    dictatorships; State repression
trauma 42, 86, 98n1
triangulation 15, 74
trust 5, 17
Type I and Type II errors 45,
    47

uncertainty 20
United Nations 32n1
United States 47
universalism 46

values 47, 48
victimization 11, 39
Vietnam war 29
violence: intra-familial 33n8, 48–49, 65, 66, 91; State 11, 12, 41
visions *see* hallucinations
voices 4, 8, 23, 79n2

wholeness 96
witnessing 42, 43, 44n9; collective witnessing 41; "reflective teams" 82, 88n2; suppression of the witness 39–41; by therapists 48, 85
women 48, 64